THE TAF

SŪRAH M

CW01499756

A COMMENTARY OF ... M

THE 19TH CHAPTER OF THE GLORIOUS QUR'ĀN

SHAYKH ABDUL RAḤEEM LIMBADA

ḤAFIẒAHULLĀH

Tafseer-Raheemi Publications 2018
info@tafseer-raheemi.com

The Tafsīr of Sūrah Maryam
First Edition: September 2014
2nd Print: Ramadhān 1439 / June 2018

ISBN: 978-1-912301-03-4

All rights reserved. No part of this publication may be reproduced, stored in any retrieval system, or transmitted in any form or by any means, electronic or otherwise, without the written permission of the author.

Author & Editing	*Shaykh* Abdul Raḥeem Limbādā *Hafizahullāh* (www.tafseer-raheemi.com)
Cover Design	Mufti Abdul-Rahmān Mangera/Shaykh Ahmed *ibn* Maulānā Mohammed Patel
Typesetting	Belal Isakjee
Printed by	Mega Printers, Turkey

Other available titles in this series:

The Tafsīr of Sūrah Fātiḥa
The Tafsīr of Sūrah Nūḥ

Available to purchase from www.tafseer-raheemi.com/shop

CONTENTS

FOREWORD 7

OBSERVATIONS FROM THE TAFSĪR OF SŪRAH MARYAM 9

PREFACE 11

INTRODUCTION 13

A SHORT SUMMARY OF SŪRAH MARYAM 14

THE TAFSĪR OF SŪRAH MARYAM 21

BIBLIOGRAPHY 158

GLOSSARY 162

FOREWORD

By *Shaykh* Yūsuf Motālā *Dāmat Barakātuhum*
Translated by *Shaykh* Maḥmood Chāndia *Ḥafiẓahullāh*

IN THE NAME OF ALLĀH, the Most Compassionate, the Most Merciful. It is an obligation upon mankind to recognise Allāh ﷻ, the Creator and Master, and to have a realisation and cognisance of Allāh's ﷻ essence and attributes. He is the Most Honourable, the Most Majestic.

Allāh ﷻ is All Aware of the shortcomings of the human who becomes preoccupied by his environment, his senses, his emotions, and what he sees and hears, despite the fact that the creation around him has been established as a sign to admonish him, remind him, and help him to reflect and mull over. It is for this purpose that Allāh, the Most Honourable, the Most Majestic, sent Prophets ﷺ and revealed books to them ﷺ.

The Qur'ān, the final Book from among the Heavenly Scriptures, which was revealed to the final Prophet and the Master of Messengers ﷺ, is an abrogating Book for all previous books. All the previous books are therefore abrogated. There is only this one Book until the Day of Judgement, which will be lifted prior to the end of time.

Humanity must recognise its Lord. If humanity wishes to accomplish connection with its Lord, then acquiring cognisance of Him is dependent on the recitation of the Qur'ān, understanding its meanings and, once an understanding is acquired, adhering to its knowledge and injunctions. No one can explain its meanings and demands except the one ﷺ upon whom it was revealed. The noble life and articulations of the Master of the earlier generations and the latter ones ﷺ are an explanation of it. His ﷺ blessed guiding statements, which have been relayed to us by his servants, the Companions ﷺ, are an elaboration of the Divine Speech. For this reason, it is necessary to study the incidents and occurrences of the time spent by the

Noble Companions ﷺ in the companionship of the master of all Prophets ﷺ. Similarly, only by studying the lives of the Companions of the Prophet ﷺ, can the life of the most honoured Prophet ﷺ be understood. The pure, sixty-three [63] year life of the Prophet ﷺ, represents a clear exegesis of the Noble Qur'ān.

May Allāh ﷻ grant us love of His Most High Essence, love and affection for the Prophet ﷺ, and a love of the glorified Book accompanied by an enamouring for its recitation.

After writing a commentary on Sūrah Yūsuf and Sūrah Nūḥ, Maulānā Abdul Raḥeem Ṣāḥib has now written this commentary on Sūrah Maryam. May the Most Noble Master, by granting an honour of approval, accept this service.

Āmīn, O Lord of the Worlds.

Shaykh Yūsuf Motālā *Dāmat Barakātuhum*
Darul Ụloom, Holcombe, Bury
2/2/1435

OBSERVATIONS FROM THE TAFSĪR OF SŪRAH MARYAM

By Apa Bint Abil Khair Hafizahallāh

THE SCIENCE OF TAFSĪR is an essential one and much benefit is reaped from its study. It reminds us of the fundamentals which form the crux of our belief, i.e. monotheism, as well as providing us with narrations of key stories and historical events.

This *tafsīr* of Sūrah Maryam and its discourse has benefited me in numerous ways. Firstly it highlights the greatness of Allāh ﷻ, His *Raḥma* [mercy], His justice, and His compassion as well as many other of His most superior attributes. Its study brings us closer to our Lord by helping us understand who Allāh ﷻ is and the meaning behind His most perfect Names. On many occasions, Allāh ﷻ is referred to as Ar-Raḥmān in Sūrah Maryam. Within the discourse of this *sūrah*, the mercy of Allāh ﷻ is highlighted in various ways, the understanding of which in turn brings us closer to our Creator. The term 'Ar-Raḥmān' has been used sixteen times within this Sūrah.

From the *tafsīr* of Sūrah Maryam, we learn about the glad tidings that are given to those who have *Taqwā* [reverential fear of Allāh ﷻ] and those who are grateful. We also learn of the warnings given by Allāh ﷻ to the disbelievers and those who reject or make a mockery of the religion. This reinforces and serves as a reminder to the reader of the power of The Almighty, and the reward of remaining steadfast in following the truth. It also emphasises the importance of keeping that hope in The Most Merciful as well as the fear and constant awareness in our Lord within our actions.

Another key message within the observation of this *sūrah* is the strengthening of the message of the Prophets ﷺ: the numerous lessons and essential reminders, and the warnings and glad tidings which all serve to help increase the faith of a believer upon the straight path, whilst also helping to re-direct the disbelievers back to the way of Allāh ﷻ and His Oneness.

I have benefited immensely from this commentary and *inshā'Allāh* I pray Allāh ﷻ grants us all the *tawfīq* [divine ability] to act upon its messages and reminders.

May Allāh Most High reward the author with the best of rewards. *Āmīn*.

Apa Bint Abil Khair *Hafizahallāh*

PREFACE

In the name of Allāh, the Most Compassionate, the Most Merciful

ALḤAMDULILLĀH, BY THE GRACE of Almighty Allāh ﷻ, the *tafsīr* of Sūrah Maryam is now ready. May Allāh ﷻ accept the efforts put into this publication and may Allāh ﷻ be pleased with everyone who has contributed towards it.

This *tafsīr* has been through a long journey. My *Ḥadhrat, Sheikhul Ḥadīth*, Ḥadhrat Maulānā Yūsuf Motālā Ṣāḥib [May Allāh ﷻ grant him a long life] instructed me to write the *tafsīr* of Sūrah Yūsuf which I did, he then instructed me to write the *tafsīr* of Sūrah Nūḥ which was published several years ago, and now finally I have also been given the opportunity to write the *tafsīr* of this *sūrah.*

It was nearly completed a few years ago. The work was then left behind. Some of it went missing too. Then my dear friend, [Maulānā] Belal Isakjee, literally pushed me into completing it.

Sūrah Maryam contains many lessons. Firstly, it has the stories of many Prophets. Stories that strengthen our hearts and our beliefs, and also teach us many lessons that we can refer to. Secondly, the main theme of this *sūrah* revolves around the Prophet 'Īsā ﷺ and his mother, Maryam ﷺ. Allāh ﷻ explains to us in the most beautiful way possible that He did not take Prophet 'Īsā ﷺ as His son; He is not in need of any offspring. All the prophets humbled themselves before Allāh ﷻ including Ḥadhrat 'Īsā ﷺ. They all knew that Allāh ﷻ was their ultimate goal. To Him they turned in supplication. In His oneness they had firm belief. They would always invite people to the *tawḥīd.* They offered their *Ṣalāh* and *Zakāh* for seeking His pleasure.

This is a lesson which humanity still needs today. This is the only way to attract Allāh's ﷻ attention and this is the only path towards solving all our problems. Read on and correct your faith. May the Almighty grant us complete *Īmān* (faith) and *Yaqīn* (belief) and keep us steadfast upon the correct beliefs. May He also give us the opportunity to write more books in the future. *Āmīn.*

I did not make my own translation. I used *Tafsīr-e-Mājidī* on most occasions. Sometimes, I combined it with A.Y. Ali's translation. Later on, Mufti A.H. Ilyas's translation from South Africa also became available and so I used that.

For tafsīr, I used Qurṭubī, Ibn Kathīr, *Ma'āriful Qur'ān*, Khandelwī, and *Tafsīr Mājidī* on a regular basis. Occasionally, other available tafsīr books were also taken into account.

May Allāh ﷻ shower His mercy upon all those who did the khidmah of the Holy Qur'ān.

May Allāh ﷻ reward all those who helped in the typesetting, page making, printing and publishing of this treatise. May Allāh ﷻ give us the *tawfīq* to do more. *Āmīn.*

Shaykh Abdul Raḥeem Limbādā *Hafizahullāh*

INTRODUCTION

When the tafsīr of Sūrah Nūḥ was somehow completed, my *Ḥaḍhrat*, Maulānā Yūsuf Motālā Ṣāḥib [May Allāh ﷻ grant him a long life] instructed me to write the *tafsīr* of Sūrah Maryam. May Allāh ﷻ grant me the *tawfīq*, assist me, and benefit us all from what will be written. *Āmīn.*

The reason he gave for choosing Sūrah Maryam is that in this *sūrah*, the story of Maryam عليها السلام and that of her son 'Īsā عليه السلام have been explained in great detail, while we live in a country dominated by Christian beliefs. There is much to share between the religions of Islam and Christianity and many of our beliefs are the same: we both believe in the same God, we believe in life after death, in God's books, in His prophets, and in His angels. Therefore, Christianity is closer to Islam than any other religion. We need to create a better understanding between the two religions.

This *sūrah* was revealed in Makkah al-Mukarramah, most likely in the fifth year after *Nubūwwah* [Prophethood]. This can be reasoned because the first migration to the land of *Ḥabesha* [Ethiopia] happened around the sixth year after *Nubūwwah*. Ḥaḍhrat Ja'far رضي الله عنه recited this *sūrah* in front of the king. The details of the migration are as follows:

We narrate this because, when a group of the early Muslims migrated to *Ḥabesha* [Ethiopia] after suffering an enormous amount of persecution at the hands of the Pagans of Makkah, Najāshī [Negus], the King of *Ḥabesha* offered them sanctuary and treated them well. He was a Christian.

The Idolaters of Makkah could not let them live in peace and therefore they dispatched a delegation to *Ḥabesha* offering the King many gifts in return for forcing the Muslims to go back to Makkah.

Najāshī called the Muslims to his court and questioned them about their beliefs. Ḥaḍhrat Ja'far رضي الله عنه explained the Islamic beliefs in a wonderful manner. Najāshī asked if he could listen to some of the verses that the Messenger of Allāh ﷺ had received from Almighy Allāh ﷻ.

Ḥaḍhrat Ja'far ﷺ recited the opening verses of Sūrah Maryam. Najāshī himself, as well as many of the priests and learned scholars who were present, started crying. Tears flowed from their eyes to such an extent that the pages of the books placed before them became wet. Najāshī in the end remarked, "These verses and the message that Jesus brought are from the same source."

Najāshī refused to hand over the Muslims to the Makkans. He rejected their gifts and showed more courtesy to the Muslims. Thereafter Najāshī also embraced Islam. When he died in the year 9 A.H. *Rasūlullāh* ﷺ performed his funeral prayer in Madīnah al-Munawwarah while Najāshī's body was in *Ḥabesha* [Ethiopia]. After his burial, Muslims of the area could continuously see *nūr* [light] descending from the sky to his grave during the night; this was a *karāmah* [miracle] of Najāshī.

His status was raised because he believed in the true Prophet ﷺ and followed him after believing in another true prophet, Jesus [Ḥaḍhrat 'Īsā ﷺ].

May Allāh ﷻ grant us the understanding of the true religion and at the same time grant us the ability to accept the truth and to follow it. *Āmīn.*

Ṭabrāni, Abū Nu'ayan, and Ibn 'Aḍī have all narrated from Abū Maryam al-Ghassānī ﷺ who says:

"I came to *Rasūlullāh* ﷺ and informed him that last night a baby girl was born at our house. He said, "Last night Sūrah Maryam was revealed to me."

A SHORT SUMMARY OF SŪRAH MARYAM

Sūrah Maryam is a *Makkī sūrah*. It was revealed to the Holy Prophet ﷺ whilst he was in Makkah al-Mukarramah. Thus the topics discussed therein are related to *Aqā'id* [beliefs]. The oneness of Allāh ﷻ and the Prophethood of previous prophets such as Zakariyyā, Yaḥyā, 'Īsā, Ibrāhīm, Ismā'īl, Mūsā and Idrīs ﷺ have also been mentioned in this *sūrah*. This is done so that the listeners [especially the Idolaters of Makkah] realise that Prophethood is not an alien thing. It is nothing that should be rebuked or refuted. Prophets have been coming and going, and were raised from amongst humanity to guide humanity. When they understand this, they could also then come to believe that Muḥammad ﷺ is also a Prophet sent by Allāh ﷻ to show humanity the correct path and to teach mankind the commands of Allāh and bring them closer to their Creator.

The belief of the *Ākhirah* [the Hereafter] has also been discussed in the last two *rukūs*, with proofs being given to elaborate the *masā'il* of the *Ākhirah* i.e. life after death.

During the closing verses, Allāh ﷻ has discussed the topic of taking a human being as a son. Allāh's ﷻ *Jalāl* [fury] is evident in these verses. He portrays astonishment at such a claim made by some people, stating that it does not befit God that He should take a son. Glory be to Him. His status is such that when He commands an act, He only has to say '*Be*!' and it happens. He also states, "The skies are ready to burst, the earth to split asunder, and the mountains to fall down in utter ruin, when people start to claim that the Compassionate Lord has taken a son. It does not suit the Most Merciful Being to take a son from His creation. Indeed, all those who are within the heavens and the earth shall come to the courtyard of the Merciful as slaves. Allāh has counted them all and numbered them precisely. They will all come to Him alone. Thereafter, whoever had believed and done the right deeds, He will create love and bondage between them." [1]

This is a brief explanatory translation of the beautiful closing verses of this beautiful chapter of the glorious Qur'ān. We will explain it in detail when we get there, *Inshā'Allāh*.

CONNECTION WITH THE PREVIOUS SŪRAH

Sūrah Al-Kahf [The Cave] precedes Sūrah Maryam [Mary] and there are many connections between the two sūrahs. In the first *sūrah*, the amazing story of the dwellers of the cave, who were made to sleep for over three centuries before being awoken, has been mentioned. In this *sūrah*, the amazing stories

[1] Qur'ān 19: 90-96.

of the birth of Yaḥyā [John the Baptist] ﷺ and the birth of Jesus [ʿĪsā] ﷺ have been mentioned.

In the previous *sūrah*, Allāh's ﷻ special mercy, which descended upon some special people is mentioned. The *Aṣ'ḥāb al-Kahf* [the people of the cave] were Unitarians living amongst idol-worshippers. They proclaimed their *tawḥīd* [belief in the oneness of Allāh ﷻ] and so were threatened and feared for their lives. They had to run away from their town and were forced to take refuge upon a nearby mountain. When they settled down in the cave, they prayed to Allāh Almighty:

رَبَّنَآ اٰتِنَا مِنْ لَّدُنْكَ رَحْمَةً وَّهَيِّئْ لَنَا مِنْ اَمْرِنَا رَشَدًا ۝

"Our Lord! Bestow upon us a special mercy from yourself, and prepare for us in our affairs the right way." [2]

As the *sūrah* proceeds, Allāh ﷻ says:

وَرَبُّكَ الْغَفُوْرُ ذُو الرَّحْمَةِ ؕ

لَوْ يُؤَاخِذُهُمْ بِمَا كَسَبُوْا لَعَجَّلَ لَهُمُ الْعَذَابَ ۝

"And your Lord is the Most Forgiving, full of mercy. If He were to seize them [the sinners] for what they have committed, then surely He would have hastened their punishment." [3]

Then in the story of Mūsā ﷺ, Allāh ﷻ says:

فَوَجَدَا عَبْدًا مِّنْ عِبَادِنَآ اٰتَيْنٰهُ رَحْمَةً

مِّنْ عِنْدِنَا وَعَلَّمْنٰهُ مِنْ لَّدُنَّا عِلْمًا ۝

---

[2] Qur'ān 18:10.

[3] Qur'ān 18:58.

"Then they found a slave of ours whom We had granted mercy especially from ourselves and whom We had taught our special knowledge from our own presence." [4]

Then when the story ends, Allāh ﷻ says:

رَحْمَةً مِّنْ رَّبِّكَ ۚ وَمَا فَعَلْتُهُۥ عَنْ أَمْرِي ۝

"... [this was] as a mercy from your Lord, I did not do it of my own accord." [5]

In the story of Dhū-al-Qarnain, he erects the huge steel barrier between Ya'jūj Ma'jūj and the people. When it reaches completion, he remarks:

هَٰذَا رَحْمَةٌ مِّن رَّبِّي ۝

"...this was a mercy from my Lord..." [6]

After Sūrah Kahf, when Sūrah Maryam starts, Allāh ﷻ says:

كٓهيعٓصٓ ۝ ذِكْرُ رَحْمَتِ رَبِّكَ عَبْدَهُۥ زَكَرِيَّا ۝

"Kāf Hā Yā 'Ayn Ṣād. [This is] a mention of the mercy of your Lord upon His servant Zakariyyā." [7]

Then Allāh ﷻ mentions His mercy on Maryam ؑ, 'Īsā ؑ, and other prophets, after which He states:

أُولَٰٓئِكَ الَّذِينَ أَنْعَمَ اللَّهُ عَلَيْهِم مِّنَ النَّبِيِّينَ مِن ذُرِّيَّةِ ءَادَمَ ۝

"Those were some of the Prophets from the progeny of Ādam upon whom Allāh bestowed His grace." [8]

---

[4] Qur'ān 18:65.

[5] Qur'ān 18:82.

[6] Qur'ān 18:98.

[7] Qur'ān 19:1-2.

[8] Qur'ān 19:58.

Thus the close connection between the two *surahs* is established through this chain of events.

In reality, the mercy of Allāh ﷻ is the prime factor due to which the universe was created. It is through His Divine mercy that it is able to keep going. He deals with us through His mercy more than what He shows through His anger and wrath. Since we have been guided to adopt the character of Allāh ﷻ, we should also show mercy in Abūndance and try to be gentle and kind in all our dealings.

Sūrah Maryam consists of ninety-eight [98] verses, seven hundred [700] words, and three thousand seven hundred [3700] letters. [9]

By reciting one letter of the Glorious Qur'ān we receive ten rewards. Therefore, if we recite Sūrah Maryam we will receive thirty seven thousand rewards.

The *surahs* of the Qur'ān are named by none other than Allāh ﷻ and His Prophet ﷺ. The names are given due to the material contained within the *surahs*. For example, Sūrah Baqarah [The Cow] is named as such because in the eighth *rukū'* of the *surah*, Allāh ﷻ has mentioned the amazing story of the murdered person who came back to life and named his murderer. This was done through the sacrifice of a cow which was slaughtered, and then one of its limbs was touched to the dead person. Similarly, this is the case for the Chapters of The Elephant, The Ant, The People, The Cattle, The Cave, The Women, and so forth. Sūrah Maryam is named after Ḥaḍhrat Maryam ؅. Her story of giving birth to Ḥaḍhrat 'Īsā ؅ is mentioned in this Sūrah. Although eminent Prophets are mentioned, *Rasūlullāh* ﷺ named this Sūrah Maryam and this name will remain attached to it forever.

A point to note here is that Allāh ﷻ has not used the name of any other female in the Qur'ān. He has named 25 Prophets and one *Ṣaḥābī* : Zaid ؅. He has used the name of Maryam more than 25 times within the Qur'ān. This may be so because in the custom of the Arabs, it was considered shameful that a person mentions his wife in any gathering. They would use phrases like, '*umm fulaan*' [the mother of my son], or, '*Bint fulaan*' [the daughter of so and so].

---

[9] Khāzin.

Allāh ﷻ mentions Maryam ؑ, firstly due to her immense piety and secondly to show that He has no wife and therefore no son.

Here I would like to mention briefly the story of Ḥaḍhrat Maryam ؑ. Her father's name was 'Imrān ibn Mathān and her mother was called Ḥannah bint Faqūdh. [10] They were both very religious and held a high status in the eyes of Allāh ﷻ. Ḥannah was childless until she reached old age.

It so happened that once, while she was seated under the shade of a tree, she saw a bird feeding her little baby. She was moved by this sight and wept whilst supplicating to Allāh ﷻ for a child of her own. She vowed that if she were to be gifted with one, she would offer the child for the services of the Sanctuary, the *Bait al-Maqdis*.

She fell pregnant. Her husband, 'Imrān, died before her delivery and therefore Maryam ؑ was born as a '*yatīm*' [an orphan]. Ḥannah took good care of her until she grew up, and to fulfil her oath, she offered her to the Sanctuary.

The normal custom was that only males were offered in the service of the Holy place. However, Maryam ؑ was accepted. All the worshippers wanted to look after her but the Prophet Zakariyyā ؑ was chosen to be her guardian because he was her uncle.

Maryam ؑ excelled others in worship. The Qur'ān says that she was from the '*Qānitīn*', indicating that she worshipped better than strong men were able to. Imām Awzā'ī رحمه الله mentions that she would stand in worship for such long hours that her feet would swell.

The angels conversed with her, and said:

يٰمَرْيَمُ إِنَّ اللّٰهَ اصْطَفٰكِ وَطَهَّرَكِ وَاصْطَفٰكِ عَلٰى نِسَآءِ الْعٰلَمِيْنَ ○

يٰمَرْيَمُ اقْنُتِيْ لِرَبِّكِ وَاسْجُدِيْ وَارْكَعِيْ مَعَ الرّٰكِعِيْنَ ○

---

[10] Ḥannah: Anna in Latin and Anne in English.

"O Maryam! Indeed Allāh has chosen you, purified you, and preferred you over all the women of the worlds. O Maryam! Obey your Rabb, *prostrate yourself and bow down along with those who bow down to Him."* [11]

Maryam ﷺ engaged herself in worship day and night. When there was some need in the service of the Sanctuary, she would fulfil it to the best of her ability.

A MIRACLE

Her uncle, Zakariyyā ﷺ who was also a Prophet would take care of her. Sometimes when he would enter her place of worship, he would see something amazing. He would find fruits out of season. He once asked her: "*O Maryam! Where did these come from*?" She replied, "*It is from Allāh. Indeed Allāh feeds [sustains] whom He wishes in ways one cannot even think of.*"

Zakariyyā ﷺ realised that Maryam ﷺ had a special status in the eyes of Allāh ﷻ.

Our beloved Prophet ﷺ says in one *ḥadīth*:

"Many among the menfolk have reached perfection. However from the women, none reached perfection except Maryam, the daughter of 'Imrān, and Āsiyah, the wife of Fir'aun [Pharaoh]. And the virtue of 'Ā'ishah over other women is like the virtue of *tharīd* over all dishes." [12]

Tharīd was one of the favourite dishes amongst the Arab community. It consists of pieces of bread soaked in a broth of meat.

In another narration, it is mentioned:

"The best among their ladies was Maryam bint 'Imrān and the best among these ladies is Khadījah bint Khuwaylid." [13]

---

[11] Qur'ān 3:42-43.

[12] Bukhārī.

[13] Bukhārī.

Allāh ﷻ mentions Maryam عليها السلام in the Qur'ān:

وَمَرْيَمَ ابْنَتَ عِمْرٰنَ الَّتِيْٓ اَحْصَنَتْ فَرْجَهَا فَنَفَخْنَا فِيْهِ مِنْ
رُّوْحِنَا وَصَدَّقَتْ بِكَلِمٰتِ رَبِّهَا وَكُتُبِهٖ وَكَانَتْ مِنَ الْقٰنِتِيْنَ ۝

"And Mary, the daughter of 'Imrān who guarded her chastity: and into whom We blew our spirit. And she believed in the words of her Rabb and in His scriptures, and she was of the obedient." [14]

As we will read in the following verses, she gave birth to *Sayyidunā* ʿĪsā عليه السلام at the age of 13. She did not marry and did not give birth to any other children. She lived a long life. She was still alive when Ḥadhrat ʿĪsā عليه السلام was raised up to the heavens at the age of 33.

She passed away long after that. Some *Mufassirīn* have said that as the unmarried women will be married in *Jannah* to the person of their choice, Maryam عليها السلام will marry our beloved Prophet ﷺ in *Jannah*.

May Allāh ﷻ shower His choicest blessings upon Ḥadhrat Maryam عليها السلام and upon her son *Sayyidunā* ʿĪsā عليه السلام.

We now commence with the Tafsīr of Sūrah Maryam.

VERSE 1

كٓهٰيٰعٓصٓ ﴿١﴾

Kāf Hā Yā 'Ayn Ṣād

These are from the *Ḥurūf Muqaṭṭa'āt* [the broken letters], which form the opening verses to many *sūrahs* of the glorious Qur'ān. Allāh ﷻ knows best what He means by these letters. However, some *Mufassirīn* have tried to understand the indication of these letters.

[14] Qur'ān 66:12.

Qatādah ﷺ says, "These are the names from among the many names of the Qur'ān." Some say, "They are the names of these *sūrahs*." e.g. *Yāsīn*, *Ṭāhā* etc.

Various interpretations have been narrated from 'Abdullāh ibn 'Abbās ﷺ, one of which is that they are from the names of Allāh ﷻ. Ḥadhrat 'Alī ﷺ would often say:

يا كهيعص اغفرلي.

"O Kāf Hā Yā 'Ayn Ṣād! Forgive me." [15]

Some *Mashāikh* [scholars] have related that at times of fear one could supplicate in this manner:

كهيعص كفايتنا حمعسق حمايتنا .

"O Kāf Hā Yā 'Ayn Ṣād is enough for us and Ḥā Mīm 'Ayn Sīn Qāf is our protection."

Jalāluddīn as-Suyūṭī ﷺ and the majority of *Mufassirīn* say, "*Allāh ﷻ knows best what He means by these letters.*"

Verses 2-3

ذِكْرُ رَحْمَتِ رَبِّكَ عَبْدَهُۥ زَكَرِيَّا ﴿٢﴾

إِذْ نَادَىٰ رَبَّهُۥ نِدَآءً خَفِيًّا ﴿٣﴾

This is a mention of the mercy of your Lord upon His servant Zakariyyā. Behold! He cried unto his Lord with a secret voice.

Zakariyyā ﷺ is a Prophet from the Prophets of the *Banū Isrā'īl*. A *Ḥadīth* in *Ṣaḥīḥ al-Bukhārī* says that, "He was a carpenter." He would work hard to earn his livelihood. He did not have any children. He feared from his relatives that

[15] Rūḥ al-Ma'ānī, Vol 16, Pg. 83.

after his death they might change the true religion. The *Banū Isrā'īl* had a habit of doing this and for this reason, Allāh ﷻ would continuously send them prophets so that their religious conditions could be rectified. Zakariyyā ﵇ wanted the light of Allāh ﷻ to keep burning bright, therefore, he prayed for a child.

The mercy of Allāh ﷻ to Zakariyyā ﵇ was shown in many ways:

[1] In the acceptance of his prayers.

[2] In granting a pious obedient son like Yaḥyā ﵇.

[3] In the love between father and son in addition to the work which Yaḥyā ﵇ did as Allāh's ﷻ Messenger for the world. [16]

"He cried unto his Lord." One night Zakariyyā ﵇ stood before the Lord Almighty and supplicated to Him with utmost humility and humbleness.

Ibn Kathīr ﵀ narrates that one night, when all his companions were asleep, he stood up and began to cry out, يا رب يا رب يا رب *"O My Lord! My Lord! My Lord!"* Allāh ﷻ replied, لبيك لبيك لبيك *"Labbayk, Labbayk, Labbayk."*

"In secret." There could be several reasons for not praying in public:

[1] At night, Allāh ﷻ showers his mercy upon the obedient servants. Because of this, the pious have given preference to this time for offering their *Tahajjud* prayers and then supplicating to Almighty Allāh ﷻ. Ya'qūb ﵇ promised his sons he would supplicate for their forgiveness at this time.

One *Ḥadīth* says:

يَا أَيُّهَا النَّاسُ أَفْشُوا السَّلَامَ وَأَطْعِمُوا الطَّعَامَ

[16] A.Y. Ali, Pg. 853.

وَصِلُوا الْأَرْحَامَ وَصَلُّوا بِاللَّيْلِ وَالنَّاسُ نِيَامٌ تَدْخُلُوا الْجَنَّةَ بِسَلَامٍ.

"O People! Spread Salām, Feed people, join ties, and pray at night while people are sleeping. You will enter Paradise with peace." [17]

In another *Ḥadīth*, *Rasūlullāh* ﷺ was asked, "*Which supplications are readily accepted?*" He replied, "[*Those made*] *during the last portion of the night and those after the farḍh prayers.*"

The Qur'ān mentions some qualities of the obedient servants:

كَانُوْا قَلِيْلًا مِّنَ اللَّيْلِ مَا يَهْجَعُوْنَ ○ وَبِالْأَسْحَارِ هُمْ يَسْتَغْفِرُوْنَ ○

"At night, they would sleep little and at early dawn they would be found praying for forgiveness." [18]

In another verse:

اَلصّٰبِرِيْنَ وَالصّٰدِقِيْنَ وَالْقٰنِتِيْنَ وَالْمُنْفِقِيْنَ وَالْمُسْتَغْفِرِيْنَ بِالْأَسْحَارِ ○

"Those who show patience [firmness and self-control] who are true [in word and deed], who worship devoutly, who spend [in the way of Allāh]; and who pray for forgiveness in the early hours of the morning." [19]

[2] Secondly, he might have feared that if he were to pray in public, people would laugh at him for making such a prayer at such an old age. Also, if Allāh ﷻ had not destined a child for him, people would tease him even more. Nasafī رحمه الله says, "His age at the time of this supplication was either 75 or 80."

[3] Praying in secret holds more sincerity and is further from showing off.

---

[17] Tirmīdhī; Ibn Mājah.

[18] Qur'ān 51:17-18.

[19] Qur'ān 3:17.

Allāh ﷻ says in another verse:

ادْعُوْا رَبَّكُمْ تَضَرُّعًا وَّخُفْيَةً ۚ إِنَّهُ لَا يُحِبُّ الْمُعْتَدِيْنَ ۝

"Call unto your Lord with humility and in secrecy, indeed Allāh does not like those who go beyond limits." [20]

And:

وَإِنْ تَجْهَرْ بِالْقَوْلِ فَإِنَّهُ يَعْلَمُ السِّرَّ وَأَخْفٰى ۝

"Even if you speak loudly [it makes no difference to him because], he knows what is whispered and all that is even more hidden [such as unspoken thoughts and desires of the heart]." [21]

Qurṭubī رحمه الله narrates the *Ḥadīth*:

خَيْرُ الذِّكْرِ الْخَفِيُّ، وَخَيْرُ الرِّزْقِ مَا يَكْفِي.

"Indeed the best of dhikr is the secret one and the best of sustenance is that which is sufficient."

This is a more general *Ḥadīth* which contains all forms of the remembrance of Allāh and includes the *Du'ā*. Qurṭubī رحمه الله says that the best of *Du'ās* is the silent one because in this verse Allāh ﷻ is praising Zakariyyā عليه السلام for praying quietly.

Ḥasan Baṣrī رحمه الله says that it is desirable to recite the *Qunūṭ* silently [i.e. in *Fajr Ṣalāh*]. The *Imām* should quietly make the *Du'ā* of *Qunūṭ* and the *Muqtadīs* [followers] should say *Āmīn* silently. This was also the opinion of Imām Mālik رحمه الله. However, Imām Shāfiʿī رحمه الله preferred that the *Qunūṭ* should be recited

[20] Qur'ān 7:55.

[21] Qur'ān 20:7.

aloud. Qurṭubī ؒ says, "This is better because *Rasūlullāh* ﷺ said *Qunūt* loudly." He is our guide therefore it would be better to follow his *Sunnah*. [22]

Note: *Qunūt* in *Fajr* is in accordance with the research of Imām Shāfiʿī ؒ. Imām Abū Ḥanīfa's ؒ research is that *Qunūt* should be recited in *Witr Ṣalāh*, not in *Fajr*.

VERSE 4

قَالَ رَبِّ اِنِّيْ وَهَنَ الْعَظْمُ مِنِّيْ وَاشْتَعَلَ

الرَّأْسُ شَيْبًا وَّلَمْ اَكُنْ بِدُعَاۤئِكَ رَبِّ شَقِيًّا ﴿٤﴾

He said, "O My Lord! Surely the bones in my body have weakened, and the head is blazing with the fire of white hair, [i.e. I have become weak and old], however, I have never been disappointed in my prayer to You.

"Surely the bones have weakened in my body." Zakariyyā's ؑ secret prayer starts with these words. First, he mentions that the bones of his body have weakened. Bones are the pillars of the body. When they become weak, the rest of the body follows.

Secondly, he says, *"The head is blazing with the fire of white hair."* There is great eloquence in these words. There is a difference between saying '*the fire was blazing in the house*' and '*the house was blazing with fire.*' Similarly, instead of saying '*my hair has become grey,*' the words chosen here portray the eloquence of the prayer. These words draw special attention and mercy upon the person who is supplicating.

Thirdly, he says, *"I have never been disappointed in my prayer to You . . ."* This means that in the past whenever I needed You, You were there for me. You have never rejected my prayers. That was my youth. Now I am old, weak, and frail. I am even more in need of Your assistance. I have high hopes in Your grace, O My Lord, that You will not reject me at this time of need.

---

[22] Tafsīr Qurṭubī.

Imām Qurṭubī says that it is *Mustaḥab* [desirable] to show humility and mention the bounties of Allāh when praying to Him. The first two sentences are to show humility and the third is to express recognition and gratitude of Allāh's favours. One person in need said to a generous person, '*I am the same person to whom you showed kindness at such and such a time.*' The generous man replied, '*Welcome to the person who came to us through us.*' Then he fulfilled his need. [23]

VERSE 5

وَإِنِّي خِفْتُ الْمَوَالِيَ مِن وَرَآءِي وَكَانَتِ
امْرَأَتِي عَاقِرًا فَهَبْ لِي مِن لَّدُنكَ وَلِيًّا ﴿٥﴾

And I fear my relatives after I am gone, and my
wife is barren, so grant me an heir by Thy grace.

"*And I fear my relatives after me.*" Nasafī writes: This refers to his brothers and his cousins. He feared that they might alter and distort the religion and would not prove to be proper successors to him. So he supplicated for a child of his own who would follow in his footsteps in the revival of the true *dīn*.

Here the word مَوَالِي has been used. It is the plural of '*Mawlā*.' The roots of this word are '*Wilāyah*' [to be friends with, to become a leader], '*Walāyah*' [to be in charge, manage, to have power, to be in command] and '*Walā*' [Devotion, loyalty]. Keeping this in mind, the word '*Mawlā*' has several meanings. In his footnotes on '*Maqāmāt al-Ḥarīrī*', Ḥadhrat Maulānā Idrīs Kāndhalwī narrates seventeen different meanings for this word. A few are mentioned here: [1] The Lord [2] The owner [3] The leader [4] The benefactor [5] The one who freed a slave [6] The helper, Aid [7] The one who loves [8] The follower [9] The neighbour (10) Cousin [11] One who has entered a peace treaty [12] Client [13] Slave [14] Freed slave.

---

[23] Qurṭubī 11:77.

The word '*Mawlā*' has been used for many different meanings in the Qur'ān and *Ḥadīth*, for example:

ذٰلِكَ بِاَنَّ اللهَ مَوْلَى الَّذِيْنَ اٰمَنُوْا وَاَنَّ الْكٰفِرِيْنَ لَا مَوْلٰى لَهُمْ ۝

"This is because Allāh is the Guardian of those who believed, whereas the disbelievers have no protector." [24]

وَرُدُّوْٓا اِلَى اللهِ مَوْلٰهُمُ الْحَقِّ ۝

"And they were taken back to Allāh, their truthful owner." [25]

وَلِكُلٍّ جَعَلْنَا مَوَالِيَ مِمَّا تَرَكَ الْوَالِدٰنِ وَالْاَقْرَبُوْنَ ۝

"And for each [man and woman] We have appointed heirs for that [inheritance] which parents and relatives leave." [26]

In the *Ḥadīth*, it is said:

مَنْ كُنْتُ مَوْلَاهُ فَعَلِيٌّ مَوْلَاهُ اللّٰهُمَّ وَالِ مَنْ وَالَاهُ اللّٰهُمَّ عَادِ مَنْ عَادَاهُ.

"If I am a person's beloved, 'Alī is also his beloved, O Allāh! Befriend he who befriends 'Alī and bear enmity toward him who holds enmity toward 'Ali." [27]

In another *Ḥadīth*:

لَا يَقُلْ أَحَدُكُمْ أَطْعِمْ رَبَّكَ، وَضِّئْ رَبَّكَ، اسْقِ رَبَّكَ. وَلْيَقُلْ سَيِّدِي مَوْلَايَ.

"None of you should say, 'Feed your Rabb, assist your Rabb in performing Wuḍhū, or give water to your Rabb'; rather one should say, 'My master and my benefactor.' [28]

---

[24] Qur'ān 47:11.

[25] Qur'ān 10:30.

[26] Qur'ān 4:33.

[27] Tirmīdhī; Ibn Mājah.

[28] Bukhārī; Muslim.

This is in reference to a slave addressing his master – so he should use the terms '*sayyed*' or '*maula*' but he should not use '*Rabb*'.

In another *Ḥadīth*, *Rasūlullāh* ﷺ said to Zaid ibn Ḥārithah ﵁:

أَنْتَ أَخُونَا وَمَوْلَانَا.

"You are our brother and our friend." [29]

This proves that using the words سيدنا ومولانا with the name of our Prophet ﷺ is allowed because he is our leader and our master. In fact Shams al-Dīn Ramlī ash-Shāfiʿī and Ibn 'Ābidīn al-Shāmi have declared it '*mustaḥab*' to use these titles for our beloved Prophet ﷺ. Similarly, the title '*Maulānā*' has been in use for our religious leaders for a long time. In this modern day and age, some ignorant people make fun of this title as well as of those to whom this title is given. These people should check their *Īmān* for they are at a risk of losing it. May Allāh ﷻ help them and guide them. *Āmīn.*

VERSE 6

يَّرِثُنِيْ وَيَرِثُ مِنْ اٰلِ يَعْقُوْبَ ۖ وَاجْعَلْهُ رَبِّ رَضِيًّا ﴿٦﴾

Who can inherit from me and inherit from the family of Ya'qūb, and make him O My Lord! Well-pleasing.

"Grant me an heir who shall inherit from me....." Zakariyyā ﵇ was not a wealthy person. He was a carpenter who had to work hard for his daily bread. Furthermore, he was a Prophet of Allāh ﷻ. The rule is that after the death of a prophet, all his assets must be distributed in charity. In a *Ṣaḥīḥ Ḥadīth*, it is narrated:

[29] Bukhārī.

لا نُورَثُ مَا تَرَكْنَا صَدَقَةٌ.

"We (the group of Prophets) leave behind no legacy, whatever we leave is Ṣadaqah." [30]

Thirdly, Zakariyyā's ﷺ one son cannot be an heir to the whole family of Ya'qūb ﷺ, because they had been spread in thousands.

Due to these reasons, the inheritance mentioned here is that of *Nubūwwah*, Prophethood.

The legacy of Zakariyyā ﷺ would be the *'Ilm* of *Nubūwwah* [the knowledge through Prophethood] and the responsibilities of Prophethood, i.e. he should be capable of receiving *Waḥī* [revelations from Allāh ﷻ].

"Make him well-pleasing", i.e. make him pleasing to Allāh ﷻ, to Zakariyyā ﷺ, and to the good people in respect of his morals and deeds.

VERSE 7

يٰزَكَرِيَّآ اِنَّا نُبَشِّرُكَ بِغُلٰمِ ٍ اسْمُهٗ يَحْيٰى لا لَمْ نَجْعَلْ لَّهٗ مِنْ قَبْلُ سَمِيًّا ﴿٧﴾

[His Du'ās were accepted] "O Zakariyyā! We give thee good news of a son. His name shall be Yaḥyā: a name that We have not given to anyone before him."

This has been explained in more detail in another verse of Sūrah Āle 'Imrān:

فَنَادَتْهُ الْمَلٰٓئِكَةُ وَهُوَ قَآئِمٌ يُّصَلِّيْ فِى الْمِحْرَابِ لا اَنَّ اللّٰهَ يُبَشِّرُكَ بِيَحْيٰى
مُصَدِّقًام بِكَلِمَةٍ مِّنَ اللّٰهِ وَسَيِّدًا وَّحَصُوْرًا وَّنَبِيًّا مِّنَ الصّٰلِحِيْنَ ۝

"Then the angels called unto him, while he was standing in prayer inside the chamber, 'Allāh doth give thee glad tidings of Yaḥyā who will confirm truth of a word from Allāh [i.e. 'Īsā/Jesus ﷺ], and besides that he will be a leader and chaste and a Prophet from among the righteous." [31]

---

[30] Bukharī; Muslim.

[31] Qur'ān 3:39.

A.Y. Ali writes: "*This was John the Baptist, the forerunner of Jesus. In accordance with his father's prayers, he and Jesus for whom he prepared the way, renewed the message of Allāh ﷻ which had been corrupted and lost among the Israelites.*"

"*His name shall be Yaḥyā...*" Yaḥyā is from حَيَاتٌ which means life. Qatādah ؒ says, "This name was given to him because Allāh had given him the inner life through *Īmān* and *Nubūwwah* [i.e. belief and Prophethood]." Some say, "Because Allāh ﷻ brought people to life by guiding them through Yaḥyā ؑ." Others say, "Because his mother's womb was brought back to life after being barren until old age."

"*A name which We have not given to anyone before him....*"

1. Ibn 'Ābbās ؓ, Qatādah, Ibn Aslam, and Suddī ؒ say that Yaḥyā ؑ was the first person to be given this name. It was Allāh's ﷻ favour upon him that He Himself named him Yaḥyā and did not burden his parents with this task.

2. Mujāhid ؒ says, "سَمِيًّا *here means resembling, likening.*" In another verse Allāh ﷻ says, "*Do you know of anyone with his name?*" Meaning he will be a special Prophet with special qualities such as leadership and chastity.

Note: Imām Qurṭubī ؒ says, "This verse indicates that beautiful names should be given preference. Arabs used to do this because a good name raises a person's status as well as reducing the likelihood of them being taunted."

'Āllāmah 'Uthmānī ؒ writes, "The prayers were accepted and the glad tidings of a son reached, whose name was already appointed by Allāh ﷻ i.e. Yaḥyā, a strange name never possessed by anyone before him. Some of the early scholars have taken the meaning of 'samīyy' as shape, i.e. no person possessing such grace and glory was ever born before him. Or it may mean that such a child was not born before that time to such old parents. Or else there was no example of his like in the past with regards to his special attributes such as tenderness of heart, weeping excessively in the remembrance of God, etc." [32]

Ḥaḍhrat Maulānā Idrīs Kāndhalwī رحمه الله writes, "Although great Prophets like Ibrāhīm and Mūsā عليهما السلام had come before Yaḥyā عليه السلام, and they were undoubtedly more virtuous than him, there has never been anyone like him in chastity, abstinence, modesty and purity i.e. Allāh ﷻ had cleansed his soul from the slightest desire of women. His nature was such that he was never inclined to women even in a *Ḥalāl* and lawful manner."

VERSE 8

قَالَ رَبِّ اَنّٰى يَكُوْنُ لِيْ غُلٰمٌ وَّكَانَتِ امْرَاَتِيْ

عَاقِرًا وَّقَدْ بَلَغْتُ مِنَ الْكِبَرِ عِتِيًّا ﴿٨﴾

He said, "O My Lord! How shall I have a son when my wife is barren and I have reached an extreme old age."

He said: "O my Lord! How shall I have a son . . ." 'Ạllāmah 'Ụthmānī رحمه الله writes, "It is the habit of man that when he hears unexpected and extraordinary good news, he repeatedly asks and probes for further satisfaction and enjoyment. This then produces further delight and the matter is undeniably established. This was the real aim behind Zakariyyā's عليه السلام asking. Ḥaḍhrat Shah Ṣāḥib says, "He was not wonderstruck when he asked for a rare object. However, when he heard that his request would be granted, then he was pleasantly surprised."

VERSE 9

قَالَ كَذٰلِكَ ج قَالَ رَبُّكَ هُوَ عَلَيَّ هَيِّنٌ وَّقَدْ

خَلَقْتُكَ مِنْ قَبْلُ وَلَمْ تَكُ شَيْئًا ﴿٩﴾

---

[32] Tafsīr 'Ụthmānī, Pg. 1380.

He said: So it will be. Thy Lord said, "That indeed is easy for me: I had indeed created thee before, when thou hadst been nothing."

He said, "So it shall be . . ." The angel who brought the good news from Allāh said that there was no need to be amazed. You shall be given a child in the same circumstances, i.e. in spite of old age, the will of Allāh ﷻ will surely come to pass.

"That indeed is easy for me . . ." It may seem difficult to you because of external factors, but it is not difficult for Allāh ﷻ. Everything is easy before His mighty power. One should look at his own existence. There was a time when he was nothing and no one knew his name or trace. His personality was called into being by Allāh ﷻ. Even if there are material processes in forming the body, in accordance with the laws of nature, the real creative force is the power of Allāh ﷻ. Therefore, one must remember that when Allāh ﷻ can create something out of nothing, why can he not then create a child from old parents?

A.Y. Ali writes, "But here, there is a subtler [deeper] meaning. John was the harbinger of Jesus, preparing the way for him; and this sentence also prepares us for the more wonderful birth of Jesus himself."

I would add to this that this could have been to prepare Zakariyyā ؑ for other miracles, such as the birth of Ḥaḍhrat 'Īsā ؑ from the Virgin Mary.

Since Yaḥyā's ؑ birth was miraculous, he should not be astonished at the birth of 'Īsā ؑ, nor should he bear any suspicion against her. How perfectly Allāh prepared him for that time.

Verse 10

قَالَ رَبِّ اجْعَلْ لِّيْٓ اٰيَةً ؕ قَالَ اٰيَتُكَ اَلَّا
تُكَلِّمَ النَّاسَ ثَلٰثَ لَيَالٍ سَوِيًّا ﴿١٠﴾

He [Zakariyyā] said, "O My Lord! Give me a sign." He replied: "Your sign is that for three nights you shall not be able to speak to the people, in spite of being in sound health."

"Your sign is that..." When you are unable to speak to the people for three days and nights, despite being healthy, then understand that she has become pregnant.

Ḥāfiẓ ibn Kathīr ﷫ writes: He requested for a sign for the contentment of his heart. This is just the same as when Ibrāhīm ﵇ said, "My Rabb! Show me how You would bring the dead to life." Allāh ﷻ asked: "Do you not believe!" He replied, "Of course I believe! However, this is for the contentment of my heart."

Regarding the speechlessness, Ibn ʿAbbās ﵁ says, "His tongue became incapacitated without any illness or any other reason." Zaid ibn Aslam ﵁ says: "He was able to recite and glorify Allāh ﷻ. However, he was only able to communicate with his people through sign language."

VERSE 11

فَخَرَجَ عَلٰى قَوْمِهٖ مِنَ الْمِحْرَابِ فَاَوْحٰى
اِلَيْهِمْ اَنْ سَبِّحُوْا بُكْرَةً وَّعَشِيًّا ﴿١١﴾

So he came to his people from the sanctuary and he gestured to them, "Engage in glorifying your Rabb morning and evening."

Tafsīr Mājidī states, "And when he came out to speak unto them, he beckoned unto them and remained speechless." [33]

Maulānā Idrīs Kāndhalwī ﷫ writes, "This could have one of two meanings: [1] Keep busy in dhikr and worship as you have been doing in the past. [2] It could mean that because of this new favour of Allāh ﷻ, you should increase

---

[33] Luke 1:21, 22.

the glorification and praise of the Lord as I am busy in His praise and glorification."

VERSE 12

يٰيَحْيٰى خُذِ الْكِتٰبَ بِقُوَّةٍ ؕ وَاٰتَيْنٰهُ الْحُكْمَ صَبِيًّا ﴿١٢﴾

"O Yaḥyā! Hold firmly to the book." We granted him wisdom while he was yet a boy.

"O Yaḥyā! Hold firmly to the book...." A.Y Ali writes, "Time passes. The son is born. In this section of the sūrah, the centre of interest is Yaḥyā, and the instruction is now given to him, 'Keep a fast hold of Allāh's revelation with all your might', for an unbelieving world had either corrupted or neglected it, and Yaḥyā [John the Baptist] was to prepare the way for Jesus, who was coming to renew and re-interpret it."

'Allāmah 'Uthmānī writes, "Ḥaḍhrat Yaḥyā was ordered to hold fast to all those Heavenly Books which were sent down either upon him or upon other prophets before him. He should follow their teachings himself and bid others to do so."

Ḥaḍhrat Shah Ṣāḥib says, "Ḥaḍhrat Yaḥyā was obliged to teach the Book to the people as his father had become quite old, whereas Yaḥyā was young."

Allāh says in Sūrah Al-Ambiyaa:

وَزَكَرِيَّآ اِذْ نَادٰى رَبَّهٗ رَبِّ لَا تَذَرْنِىْ فَرْدًا وَّاَنْتَ خَيْرُ الْوٰرِثِيْنَ ۝ فَاسْتَجَبْنَا لَهٗ ز وَوَهَبْنَا لَهٗ يَحْيٰى وَاَصْلَحْنَا لَهٗ زَوْجَهٗ ؕ اِنَّهُمْ كَانُوْا يُسٰرِعُوْنَ فِى الْخَيْرٰتِ وَيَدْعُوْنَنَا رَغَبًا وَّرَهَبًا ؕ وَكَانُوْا لَنَا خٰشِعِيْنَ ۝

"And [remember] Zakariyyā, when he cried out to His Lord, 'O my Lord! Leave me not without offspring, even though thou art the best of inheritors.' So we responded to him and granted him Yaḥyā. We cured his wife for him. They were ever quick in doing

good works. And they used to call Us in yearning and awe, and humble themselves before us." [34]

In the verse in connection بِقُوَّةٍ is generally interpreted with 'might, forcefully, firmly'. This is what has been narrated from Mujāhid ﷺ. According to Zaid ibn Aslam ﷺ, "It means learn-it, memorise it, and practice upon it, i.e. hold fast to its commands and stay well away from its prohibitions."

"*And We granted him wisdom while he was still a boy.*" A.Y. Ali writes: "*Ḥukm*, translated wisdom, implies to something more than wisdom; it is a wisdom or judgement that is entitled to judge and command, as in the matter of denouncing sin."

'Ạllāmah 'Ụthmānī ﷺ writes, "Ḥaḍhrat Yaḥyā ﷺ was, in his very childhood, blessed with wisdom and insight, knowledge, and comprehension and intuition. He was given a deep understanding of the religious rulings within the book 'Torah', and insight into the manners of service and worship.

Once some boys called him to play. He said, 'We have not been created for this.' According to many scholars, Ḥaḍhrat Yaḥyā ﷺ was endowed with Prophethood in childhood against the general custom of Allāh ﷻ."

Khāzin ﷺ says, "He was granted Prophethood at the age of three - If someone questions as to how a boy of three can be entrusted with the responsibilities of a Prophet, then the answer is that Prophethood is itself a miracle. How can a man be capable of handling the divine message of God? It is God Almighty who chooses His messengers and then grants them the ability to receive and propagate that message. Therefore, if Allāh ﷻ intends to show His power by gifting a child of three with Prophethood, then nothing can stop him."

Some *Mufassirīn* interpret '*Ḥukm*' with the book 'Torah', which means he had learned the 'Torah' in his childhood. Maybe it is for this reason that 'Ạbdullāh ibn 'Ạbbās ﷺ says, "If a child learns [memorises] the Qur'ān before

[34] Qur'ān 21:89-90.

reaching puberty, then he is from those who have been given 'Ḥukm' [wisdom, understanding] in their childhood."

Imām Qurṭubī ﷺ narrates from Qatādah ﷺ that, "Yaḥyā ﷺ never disobeyed Allāh ﷻ with a major sin or even a minor sin. He was never interested in women."

Mujāhid ﷺ says, "Yaḥyā's ﷺ food was vegetation and plants, and the tears had left permanent marks on his cheeks."

When reading Yaḥyā's ﷺ reply for the call to play, a similar story narrated by Bahlūl ﷺ comes to mind. I will narrate it for the benefit of the readers.

Bahlūl ﷺ says, I was walking along a road in Basra when I came across some boys playing with almonds and walnuts, whilst one of them stood to one side weeping and crying. I thought that the boy was crying because he had not received any almonds or walnuts to play with, so I said to him, "Son; cry no more; I shall buy you some almonds and walnuts to play with." The boy looked at me and said, "Do you think we have been created for playing?" I asked, "What else have we been created for?" He replied, 'For gaining knowledge and for worshipping Allāh ﷻ.' When I said, 'May Allāh ﷻ bless your life! How did you come to know of this?" He replied, 'Allāh ﷻ says:

"Do you think that We have created you for naught, and that you will not be returned to Us?"

I said: "My dear boy, you talk very wisely, give me a few words of counsel." Where upon he recited four couplets, which meant:

"I see men coming to this world and going away; the world and its riches are always on the move, with the wings poised for flying away. The world does not remain with any living man, nor does any man live forever to enjoy its pleasures; death and its afflictions are like two horses always running fast towards men, to trample them and to devour them. O fool! Beguiled by the charm of the world! Just think and take something [virtues] from this world to serve you in the *Ākhirah*."

After this he looked up towards the heavens, raised his hands in supplication to Allāh ﷻ, and chanted the following two couplets, with tears trickling down his cheeks:

"O Thou, unto Whom all men cry in humility, O Thou, in Whom everybody puts his trust, O Thou who fulfils the hopes of everyone who entertains good expectations of Thee, and grantest all his desires."

After reciting these verses, he fainted and fell on the ground. I laid his head in my lap and wiped the dust from his face with my sleeve. When he came to his senses, I said to him, "Son, why do you feel so afraid? You are but a child and no evil deed has yet been recorded against you in your book of deeds." He said, "So you say; but I always see my mother making a fire and she always puts splinters into the hearth first and puts big logs afterwards. I fear lest, when the fire of *Jahannam* is kindled, I should be hurled into it, even before the grown-up people!" I said, "My dear boy, you seem to be very wise, give me a few more words of counsel." At this, he recited fourteen couplets, which meant:

"I am lost in heedlessness, and death is being driven towards me, ever drawing closer. If I do not die today, I must pass away tomorrow. I pampered my body with soft, sumptuous clothes, little thinking that it must rot [in the grave] and decay. I think I see my body crumbling into dust, under the pit of the grave, under mounds of earth. My beauty will soon fade away, my body reduced to a skeleton, denuded of skin and flesh. I see the hours of my life slipping away, and yet my desires are all unfulfilled. A long journey lies before me, and I have no provisions for the way. Ah! I defied my Lord, openly transgressing His commands, while He watched over all the time. Alas! I indulged in shameful deeds! Ah! Whatever is done cannot be undone, and time once passed cannot be recalled. Ah! I sinned in secret, never let people know of my heinous sins. But tomorrow, my secret sins will be revealed, and presented to my Lord, Ah! I sinned against Him, though fearing inwardly. Trusting his Infinite Clemency, I sinned most shamelessly, most audaciously, depending upon His Infinite Forgiveness. Who else, but He will forgive my sins. Truly, He is worthy of all praise! Had there been no punishment after death, no promise of *Jannah*, no threat of *Jahannam*, in death and decay, there is sufficient admonition, to keep us away from idle pursuits. But our reason being confounded, we do not take warning from anything; and now, there is no hope for us, except that The All-Forgiving should forgive our sins. For when a slave does anything wrong, it is his Master, none else, who forgives him. No doubt I am the worst of all His men, I, who betrayed my covenant with my Lord, made in Eternity, And, it is the incapable slave whose promises carry no weight. My Lord, what shall be my fate, when the fire burns my body? The fire that melts the hardest rocks! Ah! I shall be alone when I pass into my grave. Lonely and forsaken at the time of death. I shall be alone when I rise from the grave; [With none to assist me on that day]. O Thou, Who art unique, with no partners to Thy Majesty, Have mercy on my loneliness, on my being forsaken by all."

Deeply moved by the couplets, I swooned and on recovering after a while, found that the boy had gone. I asked the other boys about him and they said "Don't you know him? He is a descendant of Imām Ḥussain ﵁." I said, "I too wondered and I believed he descended from a noble family. It is no wonder that a descendant of such illustrious ancestors should talk so wisely."

May Allāh ﷻ benefit us from the benedictions of this family! Āmīn! [35]

VERSE 13

وَحَنَانًا مِّن لَّدُنَّا وَزَكَوٰةً ۖ وَكَانَ تَقِيًّا ﴿١٣﴾

And [We also granted him] kindness and purity by our grace, And he was God-fearing.

"And kindness..." The word حَنَانْ has been translated into kindness. It has several meanings. Professor Hans Wehr translates it thus; Ḥanān: sympathy, love, affection, tenderness, commiseration, compassion, pity.

'Ạbdullāh ibn 'Ạbbās ﵄ says, "He was a mercy from us." Qatādah ﵀ goes further to say, "A mercy from which Zakariyyā ﵇ was blessed." Mujāhid ﵀ says, "His Lord showed kindness to him." 'Ịkrimah ﵀ says, "Allāh ﷻ gifted him with special love." Aṭā ibn Abī Rabāḥ ﵀ says, "We gave him special respect." Ḥāfiẓ ibn Kathīr ﵀, after narrating the above says, "The clearer

---

[35] Faḍā'il e Ṣadaqah, English, Pg. 696.

meaning seems to be, 'We gave him wisdom while he was a child and We made him a loveable person, full of purity and piety, because '*ḥanān*' literally means 'love with gentleness and affection.'[36]

Imām Qurṭubī writes, "*Ḥannān* with tashdīd is an attribute of Allāh ﷻ which means *'Ar-Rahīm* - The Most Merciful." Ibn Kathīr رحمه الله narrates here one part of a *Ḥadīth* in which *Rasūlullāh* ﷺ says, "A person will remain in Hellfire for one thousand years crying '*Ya Ḥannān Ya Mannān*.'

"*And purity by Our grace...*" The word *'Zakāh'* literally means purification. When we give our *Zakāh* to the poor we purify our remaining wealth. It also means *Barakah* [Blessing] and *Tanmiya* [Increasing].

In this verse, *Zakāh* means: 'He was purified from filth, misgivings, and sins. Qurṭubī رحمه الله adds, 'He was also a blessing for the people as he would guide them to the righteous deeds.' Some say *Zakāh* here means 'Good pure actions.'

Khāzin رحمه الله says, "We gave him wisdom in his childhood, and we made him a mercy for the people as he would have pity on their state, call them towards the Lord, guide them and at the same time he himself would practice with utmost sincerity."

"*And he was God-fearing...*" تَقِيًّا has been translated differently by various translators: [1] God-fearing [2] devout [3] pious. '*Taqwā*' literally means '*To refrain*'. Thereafter, it is used for leaving something aside due to the fear of the Almighty Allāh ﷻ. It is also used for constant awareness of the Almighty Allāh ﷻ.

Verse 14

وَبَرًّا بِوَالِدَيْهِ وَلَمْ يَكُنْ جَبَّارًا عَصِيًّا ﴿١٤﴾

He was kind to his parents and was neither rebellious nor disobedient.

[36] Ibn Kathīr, Vol. 2, Pg. 445.

Ibn Kathīr writes, "After Allāh mentions Yaḥyā's obedience to his *Rabb*, and that Allāh had created him full of mercy, purity, and piety, He adds to it Yaḥyā's obedience to his parents and his good behaviour towards them. Allāh mentioned that Yaḥyā refrained from disobeying them in speech, actions, commands, and prohibitions."

Tafsīr Mājidī states, "This is put in to refute the false accusation of sedition and rebellion brought against John by the state under Herod . . ."

Maulānā Idrīs Kāndhalwī writes that after the worship of Allāh, there is no act more virtuous than being dutiful to parents, as mentioned in Sūrah Banī Isrā'īl:

وَقَضٰى رَبُّكَ اَلَّا تَعْبُدُوْٓا اِلَّآ اِيَّاهُ وَبِالْوَالِدَيْنِ اِحْسَانًا ۭ اِمَّا يَبْلُغَنَّ عِنْدَكَ الْكِبَرَ
اَحَدُهُمَآ اَوْ كِلٰهُمَا فَلَا تَقُلْ لَّهُمَآ اُفٍّ وَّلَا تَنْهَرْهُمَا وَقُلْ لَّهُمَا قَوْلًا كَرِيْمًا ۝

"Your Rabb has commanded that you worship only Him and that you treat your parents kindly. If any one of the two, or both of them reaches old age with you, then do not even tell them 'Uff' and do not rebuke them, and speak gently to them . . ." [37]

VERSE 15

وَسَلٰمٌ عَلَيْهِ يَوْمَ وُلِدَ وَيَوْمَ يَمُوْتُ وَيَوْمَ يُبْعَثُ حَيًّا ﴿١٥﴾

And salām [peace] be on him on the day he was born, and on the day he dies, and the day he will be raised to life [again].

This means may he enjoy peace on all these days which are the most traumatic in a person's life.

Sufyān Ibn 'Uyaynah says, "The loneliest that a man will ever feel is in the following three situations: the first situation is on the day that he was born, when he sees himself coming out of what he was in. The second situation is on the day that he dies, when he sees the people that he will not

---

[37] Qur'ān 17:23.

see anymore. And the third situation is on the day when he is resurrected, when he sees himself in the huge gathering, yet alone."

Allāh ﷻ has exclusively honoured Yaḥya ﵇ by granting him peace in these critical situations. Imām Aḥmad ﵛ narrates from Ibn 'Abbās ﵂ that the Holy Prophet ﷺ said:

$$\text{مَا مِنْ أَحَدٍ مِنْ وَلَدِ آدَمَ إِلَّا قَدْ أَخْطَأَ أَوْ هَمَّ بِخَطِيئَةٍ لَيْسَ يَحْيَى بْنَ زَكَرِيَّا وَمَا يَنْبَغِي}$$

$$\text{لِأَحَدٍ أَنْ يَقُولَ أَنَا خَيْرٌ مِنْ يُونُسَ بْنِ مَتَّى عَلَيْهِ السَّلَام.}$$

"There is no son of Ādam has not erred or [at least] been inclined to do so expect for Yaḥyā, son of Zakariyyā, and it is not appropriate for anyone to say that I am better than Yūnus, son of Matt'ah." [38]

Hassan Baṣrī ﵛ says that Yaḥyā and 'Īsā ﵉ met one another, so 'Īsa ﵇ said, "Seek forgiveness for me because you are better than me." Yaḥyā ﵇ said, "You are better than me. I sent peace upon myself and Allāh sent peace upon you." This shows the excellence of both of them.

Imām Aḥmad ﵛ narrates from Ḥārith Ash'ari ﵂ that *Rasūlullāh* ﷺ said: "Yaḥyā ﵇ gathered all the *Banī Isra'īl* and they stood on a high platform. He glorified and praised Allāh ﷻ and then announced: 'Allāh ﷻ has surely instructed me with five things and commanded me to teach you these five instructions:

[1] That you worship Allāh ﷻ and associate naught unto him. *Shirk* is like a person who purchases a slave with his own pure hard earned money and then the slave goes to work. However, whatever wage he gets, he gives it to someone else. Who would like such a slave? Surely Allāh ﷻ is the one Who created you and Who provides for you. Therefore, worship Him alone and avoid *shirk*.

---

[38] Musnad Aḥmad.

[2] I instruct you to pray. Allāh ﷻ is facing a person while he is praying, therefore, do not turn your faces around while praying.

[3] I instruct you to fast. It is like a person who is sitting among a group with a bag full of musk. Each one of them is enjoying the fragrance of the musk. The smell emanating from the mouth of a fasting person and is more likeable to Allāh ﷻ than the fragrance of musk.

[4] I instruct you to give *Ṣadaqah*. It is like a person who was captured by the enemy. They tied him up and they were about to chop his neck off. However, he offered them ransom and slowly, slowly, bit by bit, he freed himself.

[5] I instruct you to invoke Allāh ﷻ abūndantly. It is like a person who was chased by his enemies. He ran and ran until he arrived at a secure fort and protected himself in it. And a person is most protected from *Shayṭān* when he is busy in the *dhikr* of Allāh ﷻ.'"

After narrating this, *Rasūlullāh* ﷺ said: "I also instruct you with five things which my *Rabb* has taught me; Hold on to *Jamā'ah* [the mass], listen and obey, migrate, and struggle in the path of Allāh ﷻ." [39]

Ibn Kathīr also narrates that Yaḥyā عليه السلام would love staying away from people. He would only feel at ease on the outskirts and in the plain lands. He would eat from the leaves of the trees and plants [e.g. lettuce, cabbages, etc.]. He would walk along the river banks. Sometimes he would eat locusts and he would say to himself, "O Yaḥyā! Who has a more luxurious life than you?" [40]

It is also narrated that he would cry a lot and that his excessive tears had affected both his cheeks.

---

[39] Qaṣaṣ ul Ambiyaa, Ibn Kathīr, Pg. 588.

[40] Pg. 589.

Maulānā Idrīs Kāndhalwī رحمه الله writes that peace from Allāh ﷻ covered Yaḥyā's عليه السلام life from all directions. Here Allāh ﷻ has mentioned three *salāms*: the first is the *salām* of *Tarbīyyah* [upbringing], the second is the *salām* of *'Ismah* [protection], and the third is the *salām* of *faḍl* [grace].

There are several narrations with regards to the *shahādat* of Yaḥyā عليه السلام. The summary is that the king of the time fell in love with a certain woman who in reality was his *maḥram* and therefore not permitted for him. He asked Yaḥyā عليه السلام who told him not to marry her. The king agreed. However, the woman began to hate Yaḥyā عليه السلام. She somehow managed to get the king to kill Yaḥyā عليه السلام. Blinded by his love, the king sent soldiers and they severed the head of Yaḥyā عليه السلام from his body while he was standing in prayer. [41]

Yaḥyā عليه السلام was martyred as narrated by the *Mufassirīn*. The Jewish community at that time had murdered him. With regards to Zakariyyā عليه السلام, there are two narrations concerning his demise with some suggesting he died a natural death whilst others say he was martyred. Wahb ibn Munabbih narrates that when the Israelites killed Yaḥyā عليه السلام, they turned towards Zakariyyā عليه السلام. Zakariyyā عليه السلام ran for his life. A tree opened up and Zakariyyā عليه السلام hid inside. The Israelites brought a saw and chopped it from top to bottom into two pieces and Zakariyyā عليه السلام was subsequently killed. He was patient. He never even uttered 'Uff' at the departure of his soul. [42]

VERSES 16-17

وَاذْكُرْ فِي الْكِتٰبِ مَرْيَمَ اِذِ انْتَبَذَتْ مِنْ اَهْلِهَا
مَكَانًا شَرْقِيًّا ﴿١٦﴾ فَاتَّخَذَتْ مِنْ دُوْنِهِمْ حِجَابًا قف
فَاَرْسَلْنَا اِلَيْهَا رُوْحَنَا فَتَمَثَّلَ لَهَا بَشَرًا سَوِيًّا ﴿١٧﴾

---

[41] Pg. 590.

[42] Ma'ārif al-Qur'ān Vol 4, Pg. 476; Al-Bidāyah Wa an-Nihāyah Vol 2, Pg. 51.

And mention Maryam in the book. Mention the time when she withdrew in seclusion from her family to go to a place far to the east. She screened [veiled] herself from the people then We sent our Rūḥ [Angel Jibrā'īl] to her. And he appeared before her in the form of a sound human being.

Ibn Kathīr writes that Allāh mentioned the story of Zakariyyā, and how he blessed him with a righteous, purified, and blessed child even in his old age while his wife was barren. He then mentions the story of Maryam. Allāh then reveals that he granted her a child named 'Īsā without the involvement of a father. Between these two stories, there is a subtle resemblance, due to which Allāh has mentioned them together here, as well as in the Sūrahs Āle 'Imrān and al-Ambiyā respectively. Allāh has mentioned these stories to show His servants His ability, the might of His authority, and that He has power over all things.

Ḥaḍhrat Maulānā Idrīs Kāndhalwī writes, "In the previous *rukū'*, Allāh mentioned the story of Zakariyyā whose wife was barren, who were both old, and yet Allāh blessed them with a child. This is amazing but even more amazing is that a lady gives birth to a child without any male having touched her. This is the indication of the power of Allāh. It is a sign of the fact that Allāh is not in need of anything at all. He can do the extraordinary and the supernatural. The birth of 'Īsā is a sign of both Allāh's power and Allāh's mercy.

By relating this incident in detail, Allāh is rejecting the claim of two groups: those who 'God forbid' claimed that 'Īsā was an illegitimate child, as well as those who claim that he was God or the son of God. Allāh says that this most blessed and fortunate child was the son of Mary created by the power of Allāh. This child is not to be worshipped, as he himself was the worshipper of God and the first words to come out of his lips were إِنِّي عَبْدُ الله – "*Indeed I am the slave of Allāh*", after which he mentioned the attributes with which he was blessed. This explained his Prophethood: that he was full of barakah, he was to offer prayers and give *Zakāh*, that he was extremely humble and obedient, and that he was dutiful to his mother. He was soft hearted, gentle, kind, and also had a nice personality. Peace was also destined for him at all three instances: birth, death and resurrection. God is not in need of peace; God is the owner and giver of peace.

Ibn Kathīr writes that Maryam, the daughter of 'Imrān, was from the progeny of Dāwūd. She was from a highly purified and devoted family among the Israelites. Allāh has mentioned the story of her own birth in Sūrah Āle 'Imrān. Her parents prayed for a child and her mother who was among the devotees of the *Bait al-Maqdis* had thought that God would bless her with a son and so she made a vow to put him into the monastery at the *Bait al-Maqdis,* where the child would stay in the service of the *Bait al-Maqdis* for his whole life.

However, when she delivered a baby girl, she was taken aback and Allāh revealed to her that this female is better than many males. Therefore, she went ahead with her vow and the child grew up in the *Bait al-Maqdis*, and her upbringing was one of the most admirable upbringings amongst the *Banī Isrā'īl.* In spite of her tender age, she was a devout worshipper, very famous for her devotion, seclusion, solitude, and asceticism. The worshippers at the Sanctuary fought over her upbringing. Finally, the dispute was settled in favour of Zakariyyā who was a great Prophet of *Banī Isrā'īl.*

As she grew up, Zakariyyā saw some amazing miracles which put this Prophet in awe of the pious young girl. Among the miracles he witnessed was the seeing of fruits out of season in the presence of Maryam. When he asked her where she had got these from, she replied, "They are from Allāh, He provides for whom He wills beyond imagination."

This is why Allāh intended to bless this extremely pious girl with one of the greatest Prophets of history, i.e. 'Īsā.

Q

Why did she go towards an Eastern Place?

A

Imām Qurṭubī ؒ gives two reasons for this. He narrates from Mufassir Suddī ؒ that she would go to one side to wash herself after menstruation. Khāzin ؒ narrates that when Maryam's ؑ menstruation would start, she would leave the sanctuary and stay at her maternal aunt's house. When her period would finish, she would wash her body and return to the Masjid. It was at this moment when she was returning to the Masjid that she saw the Angel Jibrā'īl ؑ in the form of a young handsome person.

Other *Mufassirīn* say she went to the Eastern side of the sanctuary to worship in privacy. Khāzin ؒ narrates that it was a cold wintry day so she sat on the eastern side to get some heat from the sun and busy herself in glorifying and praising her Lord Almighty.

Ibn Kathīr and Qurṭubī ؒ narrate from Ibn 'Abbās ؓ who said, "I know why the Christians face towards the eastern side when worshipping. It is because Maryam ؑ went towards the eastern side so they took that side as their Qiblah. It is on the eastern side of Jerusalem that she gave birth to 'Īsā ؑ later on."

Q

Was Maryam ؑ a female Prophet?

A

Some have said that she saw the Angel and the Angel spoke to her, therefore she is a prophet. Qurṭubī ؒ narrates from others, that she was not a Prophet and that the Angel talked to her in the form of a human being. Jibrā'īl ؑ used to come in the form of Diḥyā Kalbī ؓ before the Beloved Prophet ﷺ sometimes. The Ṣaḥābah ؓ would see him, and sometimes even hear his conversations, however, this did not make them prophets.

The Qur'ān has also said: وَأُمُّهُ صِدِّيقَةٌ – "His Mother was extremely truthful [Siddīqah]." [43]

Jibrā'īl ﷺ is given the title '*Rūḥ*' in other verses as well. Allāh ﷻ has said in Sūrah As-Shu'ạrā:

وَإِنَّهُ لَتَنزِيلُ رَبِّ الْعَٰلَمِينَ ○ نَزَلَ بِهِ الرُّوحُ الْأَمِينُ ○

"Without doubt this is a revelation from the Rabb *of the universe, the trustworthy Angel Jibrā'īl descended with it."* [44]

He came in the form of a human being so that Maryam ﷺ could see him. If he had appeared in his original form, she might have got frightened and she could have fainted. So Jibrā'īl ﷺ came in the form of a human being. Angels have been given the ability to take up various forms.

VERSE 18

قَالَتْ إِنِّيٓ أَعُوذُ بِالرَّحْمَٰنِ مِنكَ إِن كُنتَ تَقِيًّا ﴿١٨﴾

She said: Verily, I take refuge from thee with the Compassionate (Raḥmān) if thou art God-fearing.

She said: *"I take refuge from thee with the Compassionate . . ."* Maryam ﷺ, in the first instance, thought that he was a man. In seclusion, the sudden appearance of a stranger naturally frightened her, and she in turn sought for her security. But perhaps observing the *nūr* of piety and purity shining on the face of the angel, she thought it sufficient to utter these words: "I take refuge in the most Merciful..."

In *Ṣaḥīḥ al-Bukhārī*, it is narrated from Abū Wā'il ﷺ who says, "*Maryam* ﷺ *knew that a pious person would definitely be a man of understanding and logic.*"

---

[43] Qur'ān 5:75.

[44] Qur'ān 26:192-193.

VERSE 19

قَالَ اِنَّمَا اَنَا رَسُوْلُ رَبِّكِ ۖ لِاَهَبَ لَكِ غُلٰمًا زَكِيًّا ﴿١٩﴾

He replied: I am only an envoy of thy Lord, [to announce] to thee the gift of a son, pure and faultless.

He replied: "I am only a Messenger . . ." Allāh ﷻ had destined her to be the mother of the Prophet ʿĪsā ﷺ. The time had come for her to be informed of this.

ʿAllāmah ʿUthmānī ﷫ writes, "Do not worry, and banish any idea which may have struck you about me. I am not a mortal. I am an angel sent by that Being in whom thou art are seeking refuge. I have come to bestow thee a pure and clean, blessed and fortunate son from God." In this statement, there is an indication that he would be absolutely pure in respect of lineage and morality. [45]

Ibn ʿAbbās ﷠ says, "Pure in respect of piety and being clean from sins." [46] The words indicate that this child will grow up to be a Prophet and he will be sinless like all Prophets. [47]

VERSE 20

قَالَتْ اَنّٰى يَكُوْنُ لِيْ غُلٰمٌ وَّلَمْ يَمْسَسْنِيْ بَشَرٌ وَّلَمْ اَكُ بَغِيًّا ﴿٢٠﴾

She said: How shall I bear a son, when no man has touched me nor am I unchaste.

She said: "How shall I..." Allāh ﷻ cast into the heart of Maryam ﷺ that the person who was conversing with her, was really an angel. However, she remained astonished to hear the good tidings of a son when she was not married nor was she unchaste. Nasafī ﷫ writes, "She meant to say that

---

[45] ʿUthmānī, Pg. 1383.

[46] Khāzin, 217-3.

[47] Mājidī 79, Vol. 3.

there are only two ways of giving birth to a child: marriage or *zinā* [fornication]. None of them have taken place, so in what manner will I be gifted with a son. Will it bc in the present state or will I be wedded at this tender age of thirteen."

He also writes that بَغِي literally means 'to search'. A whore is called '*Baghīyy*' because she goes out to search for someone with whom she can fulfil her lust. *Tafsīr Mājidī* states, "Her words refute the most vulgar charge of the Jews that she led an immoral life." [48]

Once there was a debate on the radio regarding the miraculous birth of Jesus Christ. A Christian was arguing that his birth was a miracle because Mary ﷺ was not married. The Jew remarked, "But you don't have to be married lawfully to get pregnant." This shows that blunt manner in which the Jews accuse Maryam ﷺ of *zinā* and at the same time accuse Jesus ﷺ of being an illegitimate child. The poor Christians feel helpless and unable to respond. If this is not blasphemy, then what is it?

This accusation makes one weep and tremble, because we as Muslims believe that Jesus Christ ﷺ was a Prophet of Allāh ﷻ, in fact one of the greatest prophets to have lived. A Muslim can never be a Muslim until he believes in all the Prophets and unless he respects all the Prophets in the highest possible manner. Christianity is much closer to Islam than many people might think. We share many beliefs and values. We should be there for one another in times of need.

Verse 21

قَالَ كَذٰلِكِ ج قَالَ رَبُّكِ هُوَ عَلَيَّ هَيِّنٌ ج وَلِنَجْعَلَهُ
اٰيَةً لِّلنَّاسِ وَرَحْمَةً مِّنَّا ج وَكَانَ اَمْرًا مَّقْضِيًّا ﴿٢١﴾

He replied, "So it shall be [the command of your Rabb *will come to pass even though the means are not present]." Your* Rabb *says: It [giving her a child without a father]*

[48] See schonefields according to the Hebrews, Pg. 35.

is simple for Me and [We intend on giving her this child in a miraculous manner] so that We may make him a sign for people [by which they can realise our power] and a mercy from Us [towards who will follow him as their prophet]. And this is a decided [decreed] matter.

"*We may make him a sign...*" Jesus Christ عليه السلام will be a sign unto Mankind of the Power of Allāh ﷻ, i.e. that Allāh can create without the usual process of human reproduction. This will be a sign for mankind as a whole.

"*And he will be a mercy...*" This will be exclusively for his followers. Jesus Christ عليه السلام was an embodiment of Mercy and Compassion. Even those who followed him were bestowed with the reflection of this mercy. Allāh ﷻ says in Sūrah al-Ḥadīd:

وَجَعَلْنَا فِي قُلُوبِ الَّذِينَ اتَّبَعُوهُ رَأْفَةً وَرَحْمَةً ۝

"*And we placed Mercy and Compassion into the hearts of those who followed him.*" [49]

During the time of our beloved Prophet ﷺ, it was the Christian King Najāshī [Negus] رحمه الله who gave refuge to the Companions who were persecuted and forced to flee their homeland. When these Companions recited the verses of Sūrah Maryam to Najāshī, he started crying and tears flowed over his cheeks. Allāh ﷻ has especially mentioned this gentleness in the Qur'ān.

"*And this matter has...*" 'Ạllāmah 'Ụthmānī رحمه الله writes, "This affair shall surely be accomplished. It has been decided beforehand. There is no possibility of any reversion. Our *Ḥikmah* [wisdom] demands it that the son should be born without the touch of a man, only from the person of a woman. This will become a sign of Our mighty power for all observers and hearers."

---

[49] Qur'ān 57:27.

Imām Qurṭubī ﷺ narrates from 'Ạbdullāh ibn 'Ạbbās ﷺ who said, "Jibrā'īl ﷺ held onto the sleeve of her shirt with his finger, then blew in it and she conceived with Jesus ﷺ at once."

VERSE 22

فَحَمَلَتْهُ فَانْتَبَذَتْ بِهِ مَكَانًا قَصِيًّا ﴿٢٢﴾

Then she conceived him, and she retired with him to a place far-off.

"Then she conceived him..." Allāh ﷻ says in another verse:

وَمَرْيَمَ ابْنَتَ عِمْرٰنَ الَّتِيْ اَحْصَنَتْ فَرْجَهَا فَنَفَخْنَا فِيْهِ مِنْ
رُّوْحِنَا وَصَدَّقَتْ بِكَلِمٰتِ رَبِّهَا وَكُتُبِه وَكَانَتْ مِنَ الْقَانِتِيْنَ ۝

"*And Mary the daughter of 'Ịmrān, who guarded her chastity; and into whom we blew our spirit. She believed in the words of her* Rabb *and in His scriptures and she was amongst the obedient.*" [50]

In another verse, He says:

وَالَّتِيْ اَحْصَنَتْ فَرْجَهَا فَنَفَخْنَا فِيْهَا مِنْ رُّوْحِنَا وَجَعَلْنٰهَا وَابْنَهَا اٰيَةً لِّلْعٰلَمِيْنَ ۝

"*And* [*Remember*] *the woman* [*Mary*] *who guarded her chastity: We blew Our spirit* [*a spirit that we created*] *within her* [*Allowing her to conceive 'Īsā* ﷺ] *and made her and her son a sign for the universe.*" [51]

Exactly how she conceived is a matter which the Qur'ān does not discuss in detail. The reason being that the Qur'ān is a book of guidance and it concentrates on those aspects of the story that are necessary and which hold some form of guidance for the reader.

---

[50] Qur'ān 66:12.

[51] Qur'ān 21:91.

However, the *Mufassirīn* have mentioned some narrations which hint at this subject. Ḥāfiẓ Ibn Kathīr ﵀ writes, "Many '*Ulamā* of the *Salaf* have said that the Angel Jibrā'īl ﵇ blew into the opening of her tunic."

Khāzin ﵀ says, "He stood at a distance and blew at her." Maulānā Idrīs Kāndhalwī ﵀ says, "It should be remembered that Angels never touch Ladies." [Their condition is like an innocent baby, who does not have the slightest inclination towards either gender].

'Allāmah 'Uthmānī ﵀ writes, "Moreover, it is the action of God through Jibrā'īl ﵇."

Imām Qurṭubī ﵀ narrates from Ibn Jarīr Ṭabarī ﵀ who says, "The Christians have reported that Maryam ﵍ conceived Jesus ﵇ at the age of thirteen, and that Jesus ﵇ lived up to the age of thirty two years and a few days." Maryam ﵍ lived for six more years so her total age would be just over fifty-one years at the time of her death.

"And she retired with him to a place far-off..." Ibn 'Abbās ﵄ says, "To the furthest part of the valley, which is the valley of Bethlehem, this is about four miles from Jerusalem. She went far, in order to run away from the taunts of her people for bringing a child in spite of being unmarried." [52]

VERSE 23

فَأَجَاءَهَا الْمَخَاضُ إِلَىٰ جِذْعِ النَّخْلَةِ ج قَالَتْ
يَٰلَيْتَنِي مِتُّ قَبْلَ هَٰذَا وَكُنْتُ نَسْيًا مَّنسِيًّا ﴿٢٣﴾

The labour pains brought her to the trunk of a date palm [from which she took support]. She said: "Oh! If only I had died before this and had been completely forgotten [in that way I would not have to suffer the difficulty of being here all alone without any provisions and I would not have to worry about the insults of people when they see me with a baby].

[52] Qurṭubī.

There is a difference of opinion as to the limit of the pregnancy of Ḥaḍhrat Maryam ﷺ:

[1] 'Ịkrimah ﷺ says eight months.

[2] Qurṭubī ﷺ narrates from some who say six months.

[3] Ibn Kathīr ﷺ says the most famous opinion is that she remained pregnant like normal women, which is nine months.

[4] Ibn Juraij ﷺ has narrated from 'Ạbdullāh ibn 'Ạbbās ﷺ who says that everything happened in one instance. She conceived and delivered instantly. This is because the Qur'ān uses the letter '*Fā*' which is used for events following in succession, i.e. happening with continuity. Imām Qurṭubī ﷺ is of the opinion that this is the most correct version, whereas Imām Ibn Kathīr ﷺ prefers the third opinion, which he says, is the most famous one.

Imām Ibn Kathīr ﷺ also narrates some narrations, which say that when she conceived, she was scared and did not know what to say to the people. However, she disclosed her secret to her maternal aunt, who was the wife of Zakariyyā ﷺ. Zakariyyā ﷺ had prayed for a child. His prayers had been accepted. His wife was pregnant. When Maryam ﷺ approached her, she stood up and hugged Maryam ﷺ and she said, "Do you not know that I have conceived?" So Maryam ﷺ said, "And I have also conceived." Then she told her the full story of the appearance of the Angel and his blowing into her. Imām Mālik ﷺ narrates that once Yaḥyā's ﷺ mother said to Īsā's ﷺ mother, "Verily, I see the child in my womb prostrating to the child in your womb." Imām Mālik ﷺ says this could be due to the fact that Īsā ﷺ was more virtuous, because Allāh ﷻ made him revive the dead and cure the lepers and those born blind.

Ibn Kathīr رحمه الله also narrates that when the signs of pregnancy appeared over her, there was a pious person in the Masjid who was from her relatives who used to offer his services to the *Bait al-Maqdis*. His name was Yūsuf An-Najjār.[53] He noticed that Maryam عليها السلام had changed. At the same time, he knew the piety of Maryam عليها السلام as well as her devotion and her worship - so he was taken aback and did not know what to say. He pondered over this, and then he asked Maryam عليها السلام indirectly. He said, "O Maryam, can a tree ever come into existence without seeds? Can a child be born without a father?" She replied, "Yes, when Allāh ﷻ created the first tree and the first field of crops, it was without seeds. Similarly, Allāh ﷻ created Ādam عليه السلام without a father and without a mother." He understood and believed her. Then when Maryam عليها السلام feared the rebuke and accusations from her people, she went away from them to a place far-off; where she could see no one and nobody could see her.

"Then the pangs of childbirth drew her to a palm-tree..." She was compelled to retire to the trunk of a palm-tree, seeking relief by leaning on it. 'Allāmah 'Uthmānī رحمه الله writes, "Due to the labour pains, she went to the trunk of a tree to get support. At that time of intense pain, loneliness, helplessness, the lack of provision and comforts, and above all, the anticipation of notoriety and defamation of her religious position, she became greatly nervous and perplexed. She was so much overpowered by these circumstances that she could not restrain herself and uttered these words, "If only I had died before this and had been completely forgotten." Due to extreme pain, she did not remember those tidings, which she had received from the Angel.

VERSES 24-25

فَنَادٰىهَا مِنْ تَحْتِهَآ اَلَّا تَحْزَنِىْ قَدْ جَعَلَ رَبُّكِ تَحْتَكِ سَرِيًّا ﴿٢٤﴾

وَهُزِّيْٓ اِلَيْكِ بِجِذْعِ النَّخْلَةِ تُسٰقِطْ عَلَيْكِ رُطَبًا جَنِيًّا ﴿٢٥﴾

---

[53] Joseph the carpenter.

But [a voice] cried to her from beneath her [near the palm-tree] "Do not grieve! Your Lord has placed a brook beneath you." [A natural fresh water stream smaller than a river] And shake towards thee the trunk of the palm-tree, dates will drop on thee fresh and ripe.

We read in the previous verse that Maryam عليها السلام was so worried that she wished that she would have died before and that she had been forgotten and lost in oblivion. Now the Qur'ān tells us that Jibrā'īl عليه السلام approached her and cried out from a distance, "Do not grieve! Here is some fresh water for you to drink." He struck his heel into the dry land and water started gushing out which then flowed in her direction. He also told her, "Shake the dry palm-tree upon which you are leaning, and fresh dates will fall down for you to eat."

There are three miracles here:

[1] A palm tree is very long and hard. Even the strongest man in the world cannot shake it, let alone a weak woman in labour.

[2] A dry tree cannot produce fresh fruit. No sooner did Maryam عليها السلام shake the tree, the dates began to fall on her.

[3] This incident happened during winter which is not the time for picking fruits.

VERSE 26

فَكُلِيْ وَاشْرَبِيْ وَقَرِّيْ عَيْنًا ج فَاِمَّا تَرَيِنَّ مِنَ الْبَشَرِ اَحَدًا لا
فَقُوْلِيْٓ اِنِّيْ نَذَرْتُ لِلرَّحْمٰنِ صَوْمًا فَلَنْ اُكَلِّمَ الْيَوْمَ اِنسِيًّا ﴿٢٦﴾

So eat and drink, and cool your eyes, and if you see any human being, say: "Verily I have vowed a fast for Al-Raḥmān [the most merciful God]. So I shall never speak to a human being today."

She was then told, *"So eat and drink and cool your eyes..."* Rab'ī ibn Khuthayam says, "For a woman who has just given birth, no nourishment is better than fresh dates, and for a sick person, no medicine is better than honey." [54]

Ḥaḍhrat Maulānā Ashraf 'Ālī Thānwī writes in *Bayān al-Qur'ān*: Happiness is naturally stimulated by looking at a stream and drinking its fresh water. According to a narration in '*Rūḥ al-Ma'ānī*', she was thirsty at that time. In addition to this, things that are hot in nature are medically proven to be beneficial when consumed before or after giving birth. They serve to make labour easy, prevent excrement, and they also act as a stimulant for mental well-being. Water is hot in nature, as is noticed in hot springs, so it is appropriate at this juncture.

In addition, dates are filling, nutritious, conducive for the production of blood, and for the strengthening of the back and joints. For this reason, it is the best food and medicine for labour.

"And cool your eyes..." This means that the new-born child will be the coolness of her eyes, and a source of comfort to her.

"Verily if you see..." Ḥaḍhrat Jibrā'īl instructed her that if you see any human being who feels suspicious and asks you about this child in your hands, then tell him by way of sign language that I have made a vow not to talk to anyone for the whole day. It was lawful in their *Sharīạ* that they could observe a fast of silence. Zakariyyā was unable to speak for three days. Maybe it is from here that today we see many people observing a minute's silence upon various occasions. Maybe they felt it was impossible to keep quiet for the whole day, so they reduced it to one minute.

In our *Sharīạ*, we are not allowed to keep a fast of speech. A *Ḥadīth* in *Abū Dāwūd* says, "It is not permitted to keep quiet for the entire day until nightfall."

---

[54] Mawāhib, Pg. 136.

A *Ḥadīth* in the *Ṣaḥīḥ* says that *Rasūlullāh* ﷺ was once delivering a sermon when he noticed a person standing. *Rasūlullāh* ﷺ asked the *Ṣaḥābah*, "Who is this person?" They replied, "He is Abū Isrā'īl. He has vowed not to sit, not to take shade, not to talk and to remain in the state of fasting." *Rasūlullāh* ﷺ said, "Tell him to sit, take shade, to talk and to complete his fast." [55]

If a person wishes to remain silent for some personal reason, there would be no harm. Sometimes one has to train himself to keep quiet. A very talkative person came to the *Khānqāh* of Ḥaḍhrat Maulānā Ashraf 'Ạlī Thānwī رحمه الله. Ḥaḍhrat observed his condition for a few days, and then instructed him to write the word '*Khāmosh*' [silent] on a piece of board and wear it around his neck. So he did this for some time. When people would see him with that board around his neck, they would realise that he has been prohibited from talking to anyone. Ḥaḍhrat Sheikh Zakariyyā رحمه الله was very talkative in his youth. Once his uncle, Ḥaḍhrat Maulānā Ilyās Ṣāḥib رحمه الله said to him, "If you keep quiet for forty days, I could turn you into a *walī* [friend] of Allāh ﷻ." After a few years, Ḥaḍhrat once remembered this remark and said to his uncle, "I am ready to remain quiet for six months. Now turn me into a friend of Allāh ﷻ." He replied, "The time has gone. That was something which came out of my mouth."

VERSE 27

فَأَتَتْ بِهِ قَوْمَهَا تَحْمِلُهُ ۖ قَالُوا يَٰمَرْيَمُ لَقَدْ جِئْتِ شَيْـًٔا فَرِيًّا ﴿٢٧﴾

Then she brought the child to her people carrying him. They said to her, "Maryam, you have done a calamitous thing!"

It has been narrated from Wahb ibn Munabbih رحمه الله and Sheikh as-Sạ'dī رحمه الله that when Maryam عليها السلام appeared carrying 'Īsā عليه السلام, the word quickly spread around, and the people gathered around her. They immediately assumed the worst and lashed out towards her.

---

[55] Bukḥārī, Vol. 2, Pg. 991. Anwārul Bayān, Vol 6, Pg. 74.

When the people first saw Maryam 🌸 with the child, their immediate reaction was of shock and disbelief and they slandered her by proclaiming, *"Maryam, you have done a calamitous thing!"*

One woman raised her hand in order to hit Maryam 🌸 but Allāh 🌟 paralysed that side of the woman's body and her hand froze in that position.

Another person remarked, "This can only have happened through *zinā* [fornication]." But Allāh's 🌟 wrath soon descended upon him like that of the woman and he was condemned to eternal silence.

Then the people adopted a softer approach. And again proclaimed, *"O Maryam, you have done a calamitous thing!"*

The commentators have given various meanings for the word فَرِيًّا (calamitous), namely an outrageous act [1] worthy of accusation, [2] extraordinary, [3] major, [4] strange, or contrary to the norm.

All of which suggest their hardheartedness towards Maryam 🌸 at the time.

VERSES 28-29

يٰٓأُخْتَ هٰرُوْنَ مَا كَانَ أَبُوْكِ امْرَاَ سَوْءٍ وَّمَا كَانَتْ أُمُّكِ بَغِيًّا ﴿٢٨﴾

فَأَشَارَتْ اِلَيْهِ ۚ قَالُوْا كَيْفَ نُكَلِّمُ مَنْ كَانَ فِى الْمَهْدِ صَبِيًّا ﴿٢٩﴾

"O sister of Hārūn, your father was not a wicked man, nor was your mother unchaste." She pointed towards the child. They said, "How shall we speak to one who is in the cradle, a little child."

"O sister of Hārūn, your father was not a wicked man..." The people further rebuked Maryam 🌸 by reminding her of the piety of her family.

The name of Maryam's 🌸 father was ʿImrān 🌟 who was a very pious man and was the *Imām* of *Masjid-e-Aqṣā*. Her mother's name was Ḥannah bint Qāfūdhah whose story has been mentioned in the Qur'ān.

The people addressed Maryam 🌸 as the 'sister of Hārūn'. The commentators have given various reasons:

[1] In a *Ḥadīth*, it is mentioned that this was the name of Maryam's brother who was also renowned for his piety and was named after the Prophet Hārūn, as it was prevalent in *Banū Isrā'īl* to name their children after their pious predecessors.

[2] Maryam was from the progeny of Hārūn, hence the referral.

[3] Imām Ṭabarānī has mentioned that at that time there was a Fājir [disobedient] person whose name was Ḥarūn. The people connected Maryam to him because of the unworthy act they suspected.

[4] It has been narrated in a *Ṣaḥīḥ Ḥadīth* that the period between Mūsā, 'Īsā, and Hārūn was extremely long.

Hence, this cannot relate to Hārūn, the brother of Mūsā. Instead, As-Saddī has interpreted Maryam as being a sister from the progeny of Ḥaḍhrat Hārūn.

"Then Maryam pointed to the child..." Maryam had observed a speaking fast, she helplessly pointed to the child ('Īsā). This further enraged her people assuming her to be audacious.

They proclaimed, *"How shall we speak to one who is in the cradle, a little child?"* They were implying that, "*Are you trying to make fun of us??*"

At that instance, Allāh gave the new-born child ('Īsā) the power of speech. The words he spoke shone with truth and eloquence and eradicated any false assumptions and allegations the people had suspected or would later wrongly declare.

Imām Rāzī has stated that it has been said that when the Jews gathered around her and confronted her, Zakariyyā rushed towards her and spoke directly to the child saying that, "*If you are ordained from Allāh, then testify to your reality.*"

VERSE 30

قَالَ اِنِّىْ عَبْدُ اللّٰهِ ط اٰتٰنِىَ الْكِتٰبَ وَجَعَلَنِىْ نَبِيًّا ﴿٣٠﴾

He spoke, "I am the servant of Allāh. He has given me the Book and made me a Prophet."

'Īsā عليه السلام leaned on his left side and pointed with the forefinger to his right hand and began to answer by mentioning eight such attributes, which abolished all ill-thoughts.

The first attribute: "*I am the servant of Allāh...*" Ḥaḍhrat 'Īsā عليه السلام said, "*I am the servant of Allāh.*" This means that I am that special servant of Allāh ﷻ who was created in a way contrary to the norm, implying that I am neither the result of adultery, nor am I God, nor the son of God.

Although the discourse of 'Īsā عليه السلام whilst he was a baby took place to eliminate the accusations against his mother, he also spoke out against allegations pertaining to Allāh ﷻ. Can such a child be the result of fornication? My birth is in itself a proof of my servitude towards Allāh ﷻ.

The second attribute: "*Allāh has given me the Book...*"

Verily Allāh ﷻ will grant me the *Injīl* [Bible], which is a proof of Prophethood and is not assigned to God. Thus holding the view of 'Īsā عليه السلام to be God is once again eradicated.

Some commentators have said that the *Injīl* and Prophethood were given to 'Īsā عليه السلام in his infancy, but this view is far-fetched. The correct opinion is that these were pre-destined; hence 'Īsā عليه السلام spoke in the past tense and their reality would unfold in the future.

Qurṭubī رحمه الله has written that it has been narrated that 'Īsā عليه السلام spoke these words in his infancy, he then returned to normal and remained in his infant state until he progressed with life as a normal child. The power of speech was only given to him temporarily to establish his mother's chastity. This can be compared to the speaking of bodily parts to testify on the Day of Judgement.

The third attribute: *"Allāh has made me a Prophet..."*

This means Allāh ﷻ has predestined for me to become a prophet in the future and indeed He will give me a divine book which will prove truthful at its given time.

VERSE 31

وَجَعَلَنِي مُبٰرَكًا اَيْنَ مَا كُنْتُ ص وَاَوْصَانِى

بِالصَّلٰوةِ وَالزَّكٰوةِ مَا دُمْتُ حَيًّا ﴿٣١﴾

And He has made me blessed wherever I am and has instructed me to perform prayer and pay Zakāh as long as I remain alive.

The fourth attribute: *"And He has made me blessed wherever I am..."* Qurṭubī رحمه الله has written that مُبَارَكًا means the possessor of blessings and the benefactor in *Dīn*. 'Allāmah Tustarī رحمه الله has related that *'Mubārakan'* means, "An ordainer of good, forbidder of prohibitions, and also a guider of the stray and a helper of the oppressed."

"And He has made me blessed wherever I am..." Allāh ﷻ has made me the possessor of blessings wherever I reside and wherever I may be. This is proof that I am Allāh's ﷻ chosen servant.

The fifth attribute: *"He has instructed me to perform prayer and pay Zakāh so long as I remain alive..."* Qurṭubī رحمه الله has written: The instruction to carry out *Ṣalāh* and *Zakāh* is for when trouble befalls me or when it is possible for me to carry them out, the latter is more correct.

One must bear in mind that 'Īsā عليه السلام was raised up to the skies and will descend before *Qiyāmah*. This verse clearly points out to the ordainment of *Ṣalāh* and *Zakāh* whilst 'Īsā عليه السلام is residing upon the earth. This is because being raised towards the skies absolves a person of the Shar'ịī rulings for those living on the earth. However, when ʿĪsā عليه السلام descends, once again the rulings for *Ṣalāh* and *Zakāh* will re-apply.

"As long as I remain alive..." This portion of the verse has been interpreted as follows:

"Throughout my whole lifetime, so long as I am alive, whichever place I may be in, whenever it is appropriate and whatever type of *Ṣalāh* and *Zakāh* is being offered, I will observe them accordingly."

It is obvious that *Ṣalāh* and *Zakāh* are forms of worship and worship in itself is proof of one's servitude [*ʿạbdīyyah*], and to be a God and a slave at the same time is logically impossible.

VERSE 32

وَبَرًّاۢ بِوَالِدَتِى ۡ وَلَمْ يَجْعَلْنِى جَبَّارًا شَقِيًّا ﴿٣٢﴾

And dutiful to my mother, and He has not made me arrogant, unfortunate.

"And dutiful to my mother..." The sixth and seventh attributes are ʿĪsā's عليه السلام obedience towards his mother.

This portion of the verse indicates ʿĪsā عليه السلام as being born without a father. Qurṭubī رحمه الله has written that Ibn ʿẠbbās رضي الله عنهما has stated that when ʿĪsā عليه السلام said, *"And dutiful to my mother...."* it then became known that his existence was through the mighty powers of Allāh ﷻ in creating him without a father.

If ʿĪsā عليه السلام did have a father, then the instant instruction for obedience and *Iḥsān* [favour] would be for both, as was mentioned in the story of Ḥaḍhrat Yaḥyā عليه السلام in which it is mentioned, *"And doing good to his parents..."*, meaning that Ḥaḍhrat Yaḥyā عليه السلام was obedient to both his parents. However, this verse clearly indicates towards his mother, and serving one's mother is again a proof of one's servitude [*ʿạbdīyyah*].

"And He has not made me arrogant, unfortunate..." Qurṭubī رحمه الله has stated that the definition of جَبَّار is proud and boastful. Other commentators have narrated

that it is the one who attacks and kills due to rage. It has also been said that '*Jabbār*' is he who does not recognise another person's right over him.

شَقِيًّا means the depriver of good. Ibn 'Ạbbās رضي الله عنهما has stated that it means the '*disobedient*'.

In short, 'Īsā عليه السلام portrayed that Allāh ﷻ did not make me arrogant and foolish that I may disobey and disregard Allāh's ﷻ favour upon me. Instead, I have been instructed to be obedient towards Allāh and this is by performing *Ṣalāh*, giving *Zakāh*, and having good conduct with my mother, whereas an arrogant person would disobey Allāh ﷻ by being neglectful towards His commandments.

VERSE 33

وَالسَّلٰمُ عَلَيَّ يَوْمَ وُلِدْتُّ وَيَوْمَ اَمُوْتُ وَيَوْمَ اُبْعَثُ حَيًّا ﴿٣٣﴾

And peace is upon me the day when I was born and the day I die and the day I am raised up alive.

The eighth attribute is summarised as follows:

"And peace is upon me the day when I was born and the day I die and the day I am raised up alive." The latter part of *Īsā*'s عليه السلام speech indicates towards birth, death and resurrection. God is exempt from birth, death, etc., and is not in need of protection or safeguarding from any other source.

The entire verse has highlighted and elaborated on this point sufficiently and these were the final words that '*Īsā* عليه السلام spoke in his infancy before returning back to his former state. '*Īsā* عليه السلام then went onto progress as other children do and spoke at the same level as other children.

However, when the people heard the young child in Maryam's عليها السلام arms speak, they immediately understood it to be a proof of Maryam's عليها السلام innocence, and they were content that the child was not the result of fornication but was instead a sign of Allāh's ﷻ supreme powers. Hence, no punishment was carried out upon Maryam عليها السلام.

It has been stated in a *Ḥadīth* that after *'Īsā* عليه السلام descends from the skies, some years later he will die in Madīnah Munawwarah and be buried alongside our Prophet ﷺ.

"And peace is upon me..." The protection and safeguarding is given from Allāh on the day of death, i.e. from the questioning in the grave and further after resurrection from the fears of the Day of Judgement.

"The day when I was born..." Qurṭubī رحمه الله has written that this denotes protection given in this world by Allāh ﷻ. However, some *Mufassirīn* have interpreted it as protection from the mischievous touch of *Shayṭān* at the time of birth.

"And the day I die..." Qurṭubī رحمه الله states this denotes protection in the grave.

"And the day I am raised up alive..." A person goes through three stages: In the world they are alive, in the grave they are deceased, and in the hereafter they are raised. And in all these three stages, *'Īsā* عليه السلام is protected. Qatādah رحمه الله has said, "A woman once saw *'Īsā* عليه السلام giving life to the dead and curing the leper and lame during his life." So she commented, "Glad tidings for the womb that bore you and the breast that suckled you." In return, *'Īsā* عليه السلام said, "Glad tidings to he who reads the book of Allāh, and follows it, and practices upon it."

VERSE 34

ذٰلِكَ عِيْسَى ابْنُ مَرْيَمَ ج قَوْلَ الْحَقِّ الَّذِيْ فِيْهِ يَمْتَرُوْنَ ﴿٣٤﴾

Such is 'Īsā *son of Maryam, the word of truth wherein they are doubting.*

"Such is 'Īsā *son of Maryam..."* 'Īsā's عليه السلام eight characteristics have been mentioned in the aforementioned verses.

His speech straight after birth was a miracle in itself. *Rasūlullāh* ﷺ has said in one *Ḥadīth*, "None spoke in their cradle except for three: 'Īsā عليه السلام, the baby related to Juraij [George], and while a mother was feeding her child, people passed by with a maid. They were beating her and accusing her. She said to Allāh, "O Allāh, do not make my son like her." He stopped suckling and said, "O Allāh, make me like her." Then there passed a ruler with his pomp and glory among his servants. She said, "Make my son like him." The baby looked and said, "Do not make me like him." The mother was amazed. The baby exclaimed, "People were accusing that woman while she was innocent and pious whereas that man was a tyrant ruler."

The first words that he spoke were, "I am a servant of God." He did not say, "I am the son of God."

Now, Allāh ﷻ is declaring that <u>this</u> is 'Īsā عليه السلام, son of Maryam. This is the true and clear description of him. People doubted, disputed, raised objections and created diversions of various nature. Some made him God, and some the son of God. Some said he was a liar. Some taunted his lineage. The truth is that he was not a liar, nor God, nor the son of God, but as he himself has said, he was a slave of God. He was a great Prophet, a very blessed person, and one of the most righteous people who came into this world. His ancestry and lineage was pure and clear.

VERSE 35

مَا كَانَ لِلّٰهِ اَنْ يَّتَّخِذَ مِنْ وَّلَدٍ ۙ سُبْحٰنَهٗ ؕ

اِذَا قَضٰى اَمْرًا فَاِنَّمَا يَقُوْلُ لَهٗ كُنْ فَيَكُوْنُ ﴿٣٥﴾

It is not befitting to Allāh that He should take [to Himself] a son. Glory be to Him. When He determines a matter, He only says to it, "Be" and it becomes.

"It does not befit God to have a son..." 'Ạllāmah 'Ụthmānī رحمه الله writes, "That being whose order 'be' brings everything into existence, what need has he for sons or grandsons? Will he even experience old age or weakness that he will be in need of support? Does he experience any difficulty that he will need help? Is he in need of continuity of his name?"

If any doubt arises that naturally children are born through mother and father, then whom should we take as the father of Jesus? Then the answer is also in *'Be and it becomes'*. Why should it be difficult for that Omnipotent Being to create a child without a father? If some people were to assume that God is the father and Mary is the mother, then will they also assume the same relationship as between the parents? (God forbid). Even after assuming God as the father; the manner of Jesus's creation will not be exactly the same as that of other children - Then what is wrong in accepting that Jesus has no father and that God created him without a father?

VERSE 36

وَإِنَّ اللّٰهَ رَبِّيْ وَرَبُّكُمْ فَاعْبُدُوْهُ ۚ هٰذَا صِرَاطٌ مُّسْتَقِيْمٌ ﴿٣٦﴾

Verily Allāh is my Lord and your Lord, so worship Him. This is the straight path.

"And Verily Allāh is My Lord and Your Lord..." Ibn Kathīr writes, "Among the things which 'Īsā instructed to the people whilst he was in the cradle was that God is his Lord as well as their Lord. Therefore, they should worship Him. And that this is the straight path, "Whoever follows it, is rightly guided, whereas whosoever goes against it has gone astray." [56]

'Āllāmah 'Ụthmānī writes, "Who said this? According to some writers it is the saying of Ḥaḍhrat 'Īsā. In other words this is the supplement of his speech which began with the declaration. He said, "Verily I am a servant of Allāh, He has given me the book and made me a Prophet..." In between, Allāh Almighty mentioned two verses to wake the addressee from his sleep by saying, "This is 'Īsā, son Maryam, [and] a word of truth..." Now the declaration is being completed.

Another view, in my opinion, could be to connect it with the beginning of the chapter wherein Allāh says:

---

[56] Ibn Kathīr, Vol. 2, Pg. 451.

"And make mention of Maryam in this book..." i.e. O Muḥammad! After relating the events surrounding Ḥaḍhrat Maryam ☙ and Ḥaḍhrat ʿĪsā ☙, which have been completed, say to everyone, "My Lord and your Lord is Allāh, worship him alone. Do not ascribe sons or grandsons to Him. The straight path is that of the pure *Tawḥīd* [the oneness of Allāh ☙]. It has no crookedness in it. All the previous Prophets have been guiding people towards this doctrine. It is the people who have forged different sects and made up different ways. Now those who deny *Tawḥīd* [the oneness of Allāh ☙] should be conscious of the terrifying ordeal they will be facing on the Day of Judgement which is definitely going to come." [57]

However, this humble writer holds the first view to be more fitting. The reason is that these words have been narrated at three places within the Qur'ān:

[1] First in Sūrah Āle-ʿImrān:

$$
\text{وَمُصَدِّقًا لِّمَا بَيْنَ يَدَيَّ مِنَ التَّوْرٰةِ وَلِأُحِلَّ لَكُم بَعْضَ الَّذِي حُرِّمَ عَلَيْكُمْ}
$$

$$
\text{وَجِئْتُكُم بِاٰيَةٍ مِّن رَّبِّكُمْ ڤ فَاتَّقُوا اللهَ وَاَطِيْعُوْنِ ۜ اِنَّ اللهَ رَبِّيْ وَرَبُّكُمْ فَاعْبُدُوْهُ ط هٰذَا}
$$

$$
\text{صِرَاطٌ مُّسْتَقِيْمٌ ۜ}
$$

"And I confirm that which is before me [the Torah]. And so that I may make permissible for you some of that which was prohibited upon you, and I have come to you with a sign from your Lord. So fear Allāh and obey me. Verily Allāh is my Lord and Your Lord so worship Him. This is the straight path." [58]

[2] Secondly here in Sūrah Maryam.

[3] And thirdly in Sūrah Zukhruf:

---

[57] Tafsīr ʿUthmānī, Pg. 1389.
[58] Qur'ān 3:50-51.

وَلَمَّا جَآءَ عِيسَىٰ بِالْبَيِّنَٰتِ قَالَ قَدْ جِئْتُكُم بِالْحِكْمَةِ وَلِأُبَيِّنَ لَكُم
بَعْضَ الَّذِي تَخْتَلِفُونَ فِيهِ ج فَاتَّقُوا اللَّهَ وَأَطِيعُونِ ۝
إِنَّ اللَّهَ هُوَ رَبِّي وَرَبُّكُمْ فَاعْبُدُوهُ ط هَٰذَا صِرَاطٌ مُّسْتَقِيمٌ ۝

"And when 'Īsā came with clear proofs, He said I have brought to you wisdom and so that I may clear for you some of that in which you dispute. So fear Allāh and obey me. Verily Allāh, He, is my Lord and your Lord, so worship Him. This is the straight path."
[59]

After looking at the other two verses, it is quite clear that this sentence is the saying of 'Īsā عليه السلام. He is declaring the Lordship of Allāh ﷻ and that only He is worthy of worship.

VERSE 37

فَاخْتَلَفَ الْأَحْزَابُ مِنْ بَيْنِهِمْ ج
فَوَيْلٌ لِّلَّذِينَ كَفَرُوا مِن مَّشْهَدِ يَوْمٍ عَظِيمٍ ﴿٣٧﴾

However, the groups [among the Christians] began disputing among themselves, so woe unto those who disbelieve from the manifestation (Mashhad) of a momentous day (i.e. Day of Qiyāmah).

"However, the groups [among the Christians] began disputing among themselves..." This means that the opinions of the people of the book differed concerning 'Īsā عليه السلام, even after the explanation and the clarification of his situation. They disagreed about him being the slave of Allāh ﷻ, His Messenger, His word that He cast upon Maryam عليها السلام and a spirit from himself. So a group of them – who were the majority of the Jews – determined that he was a child of fornication and that his speaking in his cradle was mere sorcery.

---

[59] Qur'ān 43:63-64.

Another group said that that it was God who was speaking [not 'Īsā ﷺ]. Others said that he ['Īsā ﷺ)] was the son of God. Some said that he was the third part of a divine trinity with God. Yet others said that he was the servant of God and His Messenger. This latter view is the statement of truth, to which Allāh guided the believers. A similar report with this meaning has been reported from 'Amr ibn Maymūn, Ibn Juraij, Qatādah and others from the *Salaf* [predecessors] and the *Khalaf* [later generations].

Many historians from amongst the people of the book and others have mentioned that Constantine gathered the Christians in a huge assembly in their three famous gatherings. The total amount of Bishops who were gathered in that meeting was two thousand one hundred and seventy [2170]. They argued heavily with regards to the matter of 'Īsā ﷺ. They fell into many, many small groups. The largest group amongst them was a group of three hundred and eight [308], who corroborated on an opinion and stuck to it, so the King leaned towards them and he was a philosopher. Thus, he supported that group, put them ahead and threw the others out. So this group gave Constantine the greatest authority which was in fact the greatest treachery. They made many legislations for him, created many inventions and distorted the religion of the Messiah and changed it. He constructed for them huge places of worship throughout his whole kingdom, in the cities of Syria and around the islands and in Rome. The total amount of churches during his era was close to 12,000.

Maulānā Idrīs Kāndhalwī ﷺ writes that the Christians were divided into many sects. Three sects were the most prominent among them: the *Nastūrīyyah*, the *Ya'qūbīyyah*, and the *Malkānīyah*. The *Nastūrīyyah* said that Jesus was the son of God, he came from the skies and his father took him back high above the heavens. The second group, *Ya'qūbīyyah*, said 'Īsā ﷺ himself was God; he came down from the heavens and returned to his place. Meanwhile, the *Malkānīyyah* claimed that Jesus was the Third of Three. And a group from amongst them [probably the Unitarians] said Jesus was a slave of God and a Messenger of God. That was the correct Christian religion of the time. And this is the word of truth to which the Quran and *Ḥadīth* guided the

Muslim community and today there is a consensus amongst the Muslims upon this belief that Jesus was a slave of God and a mighty Prophet of God.

"Woe unto those who disbelieve from the manifestation (Mashhad) of a momentous day..." This is a severe warning to those who lie about Allāh ﷻ, invent falsehood, and claim that He [Allāh ﷻ] has a son.

However, Allāh ﷻ has given them respite until the Day of Judgement, and He has delayed their term due to forbearance, because He does not hasten punishment upon those who disobey Him. This has been related in a *Ḥadīth* collected in the two *Ṣaḥīḥs* wherein *Rasūlullāh* ﷺ said:

> *"No one is more patient than Allāh upon hearing abuse. Verily, they attribute to Him a son, yet He is the one who provides sustenance and good health for them."*

In spite of their abuse, they are invited to proclaim the truth and attain paradise, which is narrated in a *Ṣaḥīḥ Ḥadīth* narrated from 'Ubādah ibn aṣ-Ṣāmit ﵁ that *Rasūlullāh* ﷺ said:

> *"Whosoever testifies that there is no deity but Allāh, who has no partners, and that Muḥammad is His servant and Messenger, and that 'Īsā was Allāh's servant and Messenger, and His word that He cast upon Maryam and a spirit from Him, and that paradise is real and hell is real, then Allāh will admit him into paradise regardless of whatever he did."* [60]

VERSE 38

أَسْمِعْ بِهِمْ وَأَبْصِرْ ۙ يَوْمَ يَأْتُونَنَا لَٰكِنِ الظَّالِمُونَ الْيَوْمَ فِي ضَلَالٍ مُّبِينٍ ﴿٣٨﴾

How plainly they will hear, and how clearly they will see, the day they will appear before Us. However, today the wrong-doers are in a manifest error.

---

[60] Muslim.

'Ạllāmah 'Ụthmānī writes, "Today when it would be of some avail to hear and see, people are deaf and blind. Yet on the Day of Judgement, when there shall be no benefit in hearing and seeing, the eyes and ears shall be wide open. That time they will hear such things which may tear their livers and they will see such scenes which may blacken their faces. God Forbid!"

Qurṭubī has narrated from Kalbī who says, "No one will hear more and see more than them when Allāh will question 'Īsā, "Did you say to the people take me and my mother as gods leaving aside Allāh?"

Some say here, that hearing means obeying i.e. they will fully obey the instructions on that day.

"However, the unjust are today in a clear error..." Today means in this worldly life.

"Clear Error..." Qurṭubī writes: What error and mistake can be greater than believing that a similar human being, who was carried in the womb, who used to eat, drink, and pass urine and relieve himself, is God. One who makes such a huge mistake has clearly lost his senses. However, in the hereafter, he will come back to his senses, but it will be of no avail.

VERSE 39

وَأَنذِرْهُمْ يَوْمَ الْحَسْرَةِ إِذْ قُضِيَ الْأَمْرُ وَهُمْ فِي غَفْلَةٍ وَهُمْ لَا يُؤْمِنُونَ ﴿٣٩﴾

And warn them of the day of Distress, when the matter will be determined: And they are [at the moment] in negligence and they are not believing.

"And warn them of the day of distress..." The word حَسْرَة here means anguish, remorse, distress, and sighing.

'Ạbdullāh ibn Mas'ūd says, "Whoever goes into *Jahannam* will be shown his palace of *Jannah*, [which he would have received] had he done good [deeds]. At that moment he will feel this anguish and regret."

Some say that this regret will be when a person will be given his book of deeds in his left hand. That is the time when matters will have been determined. The dwellers of *Jannah* will be admitted into *Jannah* and the dwellers of *Jahannam* will be taken to *Jahannam*.

There is a *Ḥadīth* in *Ṣaḥīḥ Muslim* narrated by Abū Sa'īd al-Khudrī ﷺ that the Prophet ﷺ said, "When the people of *Jannah* will enter into *Jannah* and the people of *Jahannam* into *Jahannam*, death will be brought in the form of a ram, black and white. It will be placed between *Jannah* and *Jahannam*. Then it will be announced: "O people of *Jannah*, do you recognise this?" So they will stretch their necks and look. They will reply, "Yes! This is death." Thereafter it will be declared, "O dwellers of *Jahannam*, do you recognise this?" They will leer and look. And they will reply, "Yes! This is death." Then an order will be given for it to be slaughtered. Thereafter, it will be declared, "O dwellers of *Jannah*! Eternity and no death. O dwellers of *Jahannam*! Eternity and no death."

Then *Rasūlullāh* ﷺ recited this verse:

> "And warn them of the Day of Distress, when all matters will be decided and done with. Yet they are in negligence and not believing."

A similar *Ḥadīth* is related by Imām Bukhārī ؒ in his *Ṣaḥīḥ* and Imām Aḥmad ؒ in his *Musnad*. Also by Ibn Mājah ؒ and Tirmidhī ؒ who classed it as *Ḥasan/Ṣaḥīḥ*.

In one similar narration of Ibn Mas'ūd ؓ, there is an addition which is as follows: "...so the people of *Jannah* will rejoice with such joy that if a person were to die due to happiness, they would do so. And the people of *Jahannam* will sob and groan in such a manner that if a person was to die because of moaning and groaning, they would die."

Note:

[1] The colour of the ram signifies the state of the people upon whom death used to come, the good and the bad.

[2] Some *Sūfis* have said that the ram will be slaughtered by *Sayyidunā* Yaḥyā in the presence of the Prophet Muḥammad ﷺ. This signifies that after this, there will be eternal *ḥayāt* (life) in the condition they are in at that moment, when death is being slaughtered.

[3] This shows that *Ahl* al-*Jannah* and *Ahl* al-*Jahannam* will be immortal. Their life will be eternal. They will remain in their places forever and ever. This is the *Aqīdah* and belief of the majority of *Ahl as-Sunnah wal Jamā'ah.*

There are some who have differed in this matter. The likes of lbn Taymīyyah and Ibnul Qayyim held the opinion that the dwellers of *Jahannam* will be taken out of *Jahannam* after some time. Qurṭubī has narrated from some who went on to say that the likes of Pharaoh, Hāmān, Qārūn and even Iblīs Mal'ūn (the accursed) will be admitted into *Jannah.*

Both these views are totally wrong. The Qur'ān and *Ḥadīth* clearly explain the position of those who reject and refuse to believe that they will have to face the consequences and remain in *Jahannam* forever.

Allāh ﷻ says:

لَا يُقْضَىٰ عَلَيْهِمْ فَيَمُوتُوا وَلَا يُخَفَّفُ عَنْهُم مِّنْ عَذَابِهَا ۝

"*They will not have a complete killing effect on them so that they die, nor shall its torment be lightened for them.*" [61]

Allāh ﷻ also says:

وَمَا هُم بِخَارِجِينَ مِنَ النَّارِ ۝

"*And they will never get out of the fire.*" [62]

Note: Maulānā Idrīs Kāndhalwī writes, "The author of '*Sīratun-Nabī*', 'Allāmah Shiblī has made a mistake here, when he blindly followed lbn

[61] Qur'ān 35:36.

[62] Qur'ān 2:167.

Taymīyyah ﷬ and supported his views in this *Mas'alah*. 'Ạllāmah Shiblī and his followers gloat on their self-proclaimed understanding. The people of Nadwah take their indifferent views to be thorough research. May Allāh ﷻ protect us from the evil of wrong understanding, *Āmīn*."

VERSE 40

إِنَّا نَحْنُ نَرِثُ الْأَرْضَ وَمَنْ عَلَيْهَا وَإِلَيْنَا يُرْجَعُونَ ﴿٤٠﴾

And verily we shall inherit the earth and all those upon it and to us they shall return.

It means the ownership and kingdom of anyone else shall not remain, and everything shall return unto the Real Owner. He shall be the Direct and Absolute Ruler and Owner of everything. He shall with His wisdom execute possession in all things He wills. The goods of the world which have made you heedless shall be inherited by Him alone. The great claimants of ownership and kingdom shall be perished.

VERSE 41

وَاذْكُرْ فِي الْكِتٰبِ إِبْرٰهِيْمَ ۚ إِنَّهٗ كَانَ صِدِّيْقًا نَّبِيًّا ﴿٤١﴾

And make mention of Ibrāhīm in the book. Surely he was a man of truth, a prophet.

"*And make mention of Ibrāhīm in the book...*" This is the third story of this *sūrah*. Previously, Allāh ﷻ described the correct and complete story of the birth of 'Īsā ﷺ. Allāh ﷻ explained that divinizing a living mortal is wrong. Now Allāh ﷻ is saying that divinizing lifeless idols is also not correct.

Previously, the Christian belief was being corrected and now the belief of the *Mushrikīn* is being corrected.

The polytheists of Makkah used to boast that they are the children of Ibrāhīm ﷺ and held his creed. They are informed here of the role of their father against idolatry.

Ibrāhīm عليه السلام lived in Babylon. He was a believer in one God. He called his father, his people, and the king Nimrūd towards this belief. He explained the falsehood of idol-worship. He was persecuted and forced to abandon his home town in order to protect his belief. He had to offer huge sacrifices to preserve his belief.

'Allāmah as-Suyūṭī رحمه الله has written that Ibrāhīm عليه السلام lived for 175 years. The period between him and Ādam عليه السلام is 2000 years and between him and Nūḥ عليه السلام is 1000 years. [63]

"Verily he was a man of truth, a prophet..." صِدِّيق means a teller of truth who testifies his words by actions, or it means that righteous good natured soul who bears a very high capacity of absorbing the truth; what he receives from God, goes into the bottom of his heart without prevarication, leaving no room for doubt and suspicion. Ibrāhīm عليه السلام was a '*Siddīq*' by all manners. And because Prophethood is not essential for righteousness [as it is a special gift from Allāh تعالى] the word 'Prophet' is also added to confirm his Prophethood.

VERSE 42

إِذْ قَالَ لِأَبِيهِ يَٰٓأَبَتِ لِمَ تَعْبُدُ مَا لَا
يَسْمَعُ وَلَا يُبْصِرُ وَلَا يُغْنِى عَنكَ شَيْـًٔا ﴿٤٢﴾

When he said to his father: "Dear father! Why do you worship that which neither hears nor sees, nor avails you in anyway."

"When he said to his father: "Dear father..." In Arabic, the words يَا أَبَتِ convey deep respect and intense love for one's father. Allāh تعالى had instilled in the nature of Ibrāhīm عليه السلام all good characteristics and noble qualities.

Tafsīr Mawāhib Ar-Raḥmān discusses the name of Ibrāhīm's father at this juncture. The author narrates two opinions regarding this:

---

[63] Ma'ārif Kāndhalwī.

[1] Āzar. The Qur'ān says:

وَاِذْ قَالَ اِبْرٰهِيْمُ لِاَبِيْهِ اٰزَرَ ۝

"When Ibrāhīm said to his father, Āzar." [64]

[2] Tārakh. As-Suyūṭī ﷺ and others have said that Āzar was the name of his uncle. Ibrāhīm's ﷺ father had died and Āzar took care of his nephew after him. For this reason, Āzar was referred to as father in the verse of An'ām.

However, Maulānā Amīr 'Ạlī Ṣāḥib says that this is incorrect. It appears that Tārakh and Āzar are both names of the same person. Perhaps one is a name, the other a cognomen. The reason is that after a few verses, Ibrāhīm ﷺ said, "And I Will seek forgiveness for you from my *Rabb*." Also he says, "And forgive my father; he has been from the misguided people" and "O my Lord, forgive me and my parents and all the believers the day when the reckoning takes place."

Thereafter, the *Ḥadīth* says that, 'Ibrāhīm will meet his father Āzar on the day of Judgement . . .' Therefore the first view seems to be more correct.

"Why do you worship ..." The word "*Ịbādah*' [worship] means humility and humbleness at its peak. When a person worships someone, it means he has totally submitted himself and lowered himself to him.

If we ponder over this, we will realise that this is not possible with idols. Firstly, when the worshipper humbles himself before the worshipped, it must be to show gratitude to the favours, bounties, and blessings showered by the worshipped upon the worshipper. Here, the idols are lifeless and do not have the ability to bless someone with something, so why should they be worshipped?

Secondly, the intention of the worshipper is to supplicate, and seek help from the worshipped. That is why a *Ḥadīth* says, "*Du'ā* is the essence of

---

[64] Qur'ān 6:74.

'*Ibādah.*" With the idols, a person can sit all day and night asking them, but they will not hear a single word nor will they reply. Therefore, what is the point of worshipping them? Maybe this is why Ibrāhīm ﷺ said, 'that which does not hear nor see'.

Thirdly, the idol-worshipper is superior to the idols, because he has the capacity to see, hear, walk, and talk and is able to conduct his affairs. Whereas the idols have been crafted and created by man. They are inferior to the human being. Therefore, how can the one who is better and superior bow down in front of the one who is lower and inferior?

Fourthly, the idols cannot avert any harm from themselves. If someone was to break them or snatch the food which was put before them, they would not be able to protect themselves nor their food. Allāh ﷻ says in Sūrah al-Ḥajj:

إِنَّ الَّذِيْنَ تَدْعُوْنَ مِنْ دُوْنِ اللهِ لَنْ يَّخْلُقُوْا ذُبَابًا وَّلَوِ اجْتَمَعُوْا لَهٗ ط
وَإِنْ يَّسْلُبْهُمُ الذُّبَابُ شَيْئًا لَّا يَسْتَنْقِذُوْهُ مِنْهُ ط ضَعُفَ الطَّالِبُ وَالْمَطْلُوْبُ ۝
مَا قَدَرُوا اللهَ حَقَّ قَدْرِهِ ط إِنَّ اللهَ لَقَوِيٌّ عَزِيْزٌ ۝

"*Those whom you call upon besides Allāh [the idols] can never create a fly even if they were all to get together. And if a fly were to snatch something from them they would not be able to save it from them. Weak is the seeker and the sought. [Surely] they did not value Allāh as He should be valued. Verily Allāh is powerful, mighty.*"[65]

VERSE 43

يٰاَبَتِ اِنِّىْ قَدْ جَاءَنِىْ مِنَ الْعِلْمِ مَا لَمْ
يَأْتِكَ فَاتَّبِعْنِىْ اَهْدِكَ صِرَاطًا سَوِيًّا ﴿٤٣﴾

Dear Father, such knowledge has come to me that has not come to you so follow me and I shall show you the straight path.

[65] Qur'ān 22:73-74.

Tafsīr Mājidī states that the term knowledge here means the divine revelation which is the only infallible knowledge.

Ḥadhrat Maulānā Idrīs Kāndhalwī رحمه الله writes that a non-*ʿālim* [scholar] should follow an *ʿālim*. *Ittibā*ʼ means to walk behind someone. Ibrāhīm عليه السلام is trying to say, "Dear Father, follow me in my footsteps, *Inshā'-Allāh*, I will help you to reach God Almighty. Being a father, you have rights upon me and, being a son, I love you. For that reason, I am requesting you to follow me. The *ʿIlm* [Knowledge] which I have received is directly from God Almighty. There is no possibility of mistakes in it and following such knowledge is logical.

Verse 44

يٰٓاَبَتِ لَا تَعْبُدِ الشَّيْطٰنَ ۭ اِنَّ الشَّيْطٰنَ كَانَ لِلرَّحْمٰنِ عَصِيًّا ﴿٤٤﴾

Dear Father, do not worship Shayṭān. Indeed he was ever disobedient to Raḥmān.

The third point which Ibrāhīm عليه السلام made clear was that one should not worship *Shayṭān*. This is because worshipping idols is in reality worshipping *Shayṭān* because idols are lifeless. They cannot speak. They cannot invite anyone towards their worship. This invitation was made to them by *Shayṭān*. As in another place, Allāh تعالى said:

وَزَيَّنَ لَهُمُ الشَّيْطٰنُ اَعْمَالَهُمْ فَصَدَّهُمْ عَنِ السَّبِيْلِ فَهُمْ لَا يَهْتَدُوْنَ ۝

"Shayṭān has beautified their actions for them and prevented them from the right path. Because of which they are not rightly guided." [66]

Shayṭān is the greatest disobedient to Allāh تعالى. He refused to prostrate to Ādam عليه السلام and thus was rejected by Allāh تعالى and he made a firm resolution to mislead the progeny of the Children of Ādam.

[66] Qur'ān 27:24.

VERSE 45

يٰٓاَبَتِ اِنِّىْٓ اَخَافُ اَنْ يَّمَسَّكَ عَذَابٌ مِّنَ الرَّحْمٰنِ فَتَكُوْنَ لِلشَّيْطٰنِ وَلِيًّا ﴿٤٥﴾

Dear Father, Indeed I fear that a punishment would afflict you from Ar-Raḥmān [The Compassionate One], after which you would be a companion of Shayṭān.

The fourth point which Ibrāhīm ﷺ mentioned was, "Dear Father, if you continue with your polytheism and disobedience, then you are at great risk of some form of punishment from Allāh ﷻ who in reality is the most Merciful. However, your continuous disobedience will attract His wrath, then you will have no protector nor any helper."

Tafsīr Mājidī states that this means a punishment could afflict you in this world and then you could become *Shayṭān's* companion in the hereafter i.e. in the hell fire. Ḥadhrat Maulānā 'Abdul Mājid ﷫ narrates these words from the Bible which I quote from Polano, "Woe to my father and to this evil generation: Woe to those who incline their hearts to vanity and worship senseless images without the power to smell or eat, to see or hear. Mouth they have, but sounds they cannot utter; eyes they have, but lack all the power to see: they have ears that cannot hear, hands that cannot move, and feet that cannot walk. Senseless as they are the men who wrought them, senseless all who trust in them and bow before them . . . then why serve senseless, powerless gods – gods who can neither help thee in thy need nor hear thy supplications? Evil it is of thee and those who unite with thee to serve images of stone and wood, forgetting the lord God who made the heaven and the earth and all that is therein. Ye bring guilt upon your souls, the same guilt for which your ancestors were punished by waters of the flood. Cease, O my Father, to serve such Gods, lest evil fall upon thy soul and the souls of all thy family." [67]

Tafsīr Nasafī states, "Look at the beautiful manner of Ibrāhīm's ﷺ advice, his soft approach, his good character, etc."

---

[67] Polano pp. 35-36; Tafsīr Mājidī, Vol 3, Pg. 84-85.

One *Ḥadīth* says that Ibrāhīm عليه السلام was instructed by Allāh ﷻ that you are my *Khalīl* [friend] so behave in a goodly manner even with the *Kuffār* (disbelievers); you will enter the places of *Al-Abrār.*

Firstly, he looked for the reason behind his father's mistake and woke him up from his sleep, because if a person was to worship the best of creation in the eyes of the creator i.e. the prophets, then this person too would be in clear misguidance. So what would you say about a person who worships a stone or a tree which cannot hear the worshipper nor see the true essence of his worship and cannot fulfil any need nor remove any problems?

Thereafter, in the second sentence, he invited him towards the truth in a gentle manner. He did not say to his father, 'You are a *jāhil* and I am an *'ālim'*. Rather, he said, 'I have a little bit of knowledge which you don't have so I want you to benefit from that knowledge and turn towards the straight path. Let's say if we were both travelling and you lost the way but I knew the way out, would you not follow me to save yourself from destruction in bewilderment? Of course you would, so the case here is the same.'

Thirdly, Ibrāhīm عليه السلام instructed him that it's *Shayṭān* who is making you do these things, who is beautifying idol worship to you, so you should give up your friendship with *Shayṭān* and make friendship with *Ar-Raḥmān.*

Then fourthly and finally, Ibrāhīm عليه السلام warned him of the evil fate which he would have to suffer and the destruction he was facing. However, he held onto the good manners in a sense that he did not say clearly that you will be punished, rather he said, I fear that punishment could come towards you. Moreover, he started off every *naṣīḥah* [advice] with يَٰٓأَبَتِ which means 'Dear father, Dear father'. Here is an indication that a person should respect his father even if he was a *Kāfir.*

VERSE 46

قَالَ أَرَاغِبٌ أَنتَ عَنْ ءَالِهَتِى يَٰٓإِبْرَٰهِيمُ ج
لَئِن لَّمْ تَنتَهِ لَأَرْجُمَنَّكَ وَٱهْجُرْنِى مَلِيًّا ﴿٤٦﴾

He said: O Ibrāhīm! Are you one who turns away from my Gods? If you do not desist, I shall stone you. And leave me for a long period.

"He said: O Ibrāhīm..." The father hearing the speech of Sayyidunā Ibrāhīm ﷺ said, "It seems that you have become a heretic and you disbelieve in our gods. Now leave your unbelief and heresy, otherwise, I will stone you to death with my own hands. If you want to stay alive, then leave us alone or go away from here, I do not want to see your face for the rest of my life. Go away before I take any action." [68]

By narrating these words, Allāh ﷻ is consoling our beloved Prophet ﷺ, because he was constantly pestered and harassed by his uncle Abū Lahab and so Allāh ﷻ informs him that your great, great grandfather Ibrāhīm ﷺ was scolded by his own father. When he showed *ṣabr* and patience, you must also hold on to *ṣabr* and patience. [69]

Verse 47

قَالَ سَلٰمٌ عَلَيْكَ ج سَاَسْتَغْفِرُ لَكَ رَبِّىْ ط اِنَّهٗ كَانَ بِىْ حَفِيًّا ﴿٤٧﴾

He [Ibrāhīm] said: Peace be on you; I will ask for forgiveness for you from my Lord. Surely He has been ever so kind to me.

"Ibrāhīm said: Peace be upon you..." This *salām* is known as the *salām* of separation. In other words, 'if you want it that way, then goodbye.' In another place Allāh ﷻ says:

وَاِذَا سَمِعُوا اللَّغْوَ اَعْرَضُوْا عَنْهُ وَقَالُوْا لَنَا اَعْمَالُنَا

وَلَكُمْ اَعْمَالُكُمْ ز سَلٰمٌ عَلَيْكُمْ ز لَا نَبْتَغِى الْجٰهِلِيْنَ ۝

"And when they hear vain talk they turn away from it and say, 'For us our deeds and for you your deeds', Peace be upon you, we do not seek the ignorant." [70]

---

[68] 'Uthmānī, Pg. 1392.

[69] Mawāhib, Pg. 162.

[70] Qur'ān 28:55.

This shows that if a relative turns against the command of Allāh ﷻ and argues about it, then it is permissible to disassociate from them. It also shows that to repel evil with virtue is from the characteristics of the Prophets. [71]

Ḥaḍhrat Shah Ṣāḥib رحمه الله writes, "We understand from here that if the parents are displeased with the religious mind of the son and they throw him out of the house, if the son goes away saying some sweet words to the parents, then that son will not be regarded as undutiful." [72]

Sometimes it becomes necessary to detach from one's relatives for the sake of preserving the *Dīn*. One young man turned pious and started praying five times a day. His father said, 'leave your prayers and stand in the shop, you can pray when you become old and have a white beard.' Another friend told me, 'I want to keep a beard, but my parents won't let me.'

Many young converts are driven out of their homes for embracing Islam. They should remember Ibrāhīm عليه السلام and never show anger. Rather they should become more humble and serve their parents more and tell them that this servitude which I am showing is the teaching of Islam. In other words, I am being more dutiful because Islam teaches me to do so. In this way, they might also develop the love of Islam and perhaps Allāh ﷻ might give *Hidāyah* to them as well.

Some *Mufassirīn* have said that the words '*Peace be upon you*' are in a literal sense i.e. Ibrāhīm عليه السلام is actually praying for his father. He did promise to seek forgiveness for him so he made Du'ā of peace for him as well. It is a sign of godliness that praise and insult become equal in the eyes of a person, i.e. he prays for the one who praises him as well as for one who insults him.

Imām Qurṭubī رحمه الله has touched here on the *mas'alah* of saying *salām* to a non-Muslim. He writes:

Sufyān ibn 'Ụyaynah رحمه الله was asked, "Is it permissible to say *salām* to a non-believer?" He replied, "Yes. Allāh ﷻ has said, "Allāh ﷻ does not prevent you from showing kindness and being just with those who have not fought you in

[71] Mawāhib, Pg. 163.

[72] 'Ụthmānī, 1393.

your *Dīn* [faith] nor have they driven you away from your homes. Verily Allāh ﷻ loves those who are just." Allāh ﷻ has also said, "Surely you have a good example in Ibrāhīm ﷺ and those with him." And Ibrāhīm ﷺ said, "Peace be upon you."

With regards to this, there are two narrations:

[1] "Do not rush to say *salāms* to the Jews or Christians." The reason for this could be explained from another *Ḥadīth* which says, 'When Jews greet you, they say '*Assāmu 'Ạlaykum*', so in reply say, 'And upon you too.' This means that they would omit the 'L' and instead of '*salām*' (peace), they would say '*sām'* which in Hebrew means 'death'. Therefore, they would be cursing the Muslims meaning 'May you die'. This could explain why the Prophet ﷺ prohibited greeting the Jews of that time.

[2] Another lengthy *Ḥadīth* says that once *Rasūlullāh* ﷺ passed by a gathering wherein there was a mixture of Muslims, Jews, and *Mushrikīn*. He said to them, '*Assalāmu 'Ạlaykum*'.

Ibrāhīm Nakha'ī ؒ says, "If there is any necessity in saying *salām* to a non-Muslim then do so."

Ibn Mas'ūd ؓ was travelling when a *Dehqān* [leader of non-Muslims] gave him company. He said *salām* to him. Ạlqamah ؒ, his student asked, 'Is it not *makrūh* to rush into saying *salām* to them?" He replied: "Yes, but this is the right of company," [*Ḥaqq As-ṣuḥbah*].

When Abū Umāmah ؓ would return home, he would not pass by any person without greeting him, whether he was Muslim or Christian, young or old. Someone questioned him to which he replied, "We have been instructed to spread *salām*."

Imām Awzā'ī ؒ was asked and he replied, "If you greet, righteous men before you have greeted, and if you don't greet, some have not greeted." Ḥasan Baṣrī ؒ says, "If you pass by a gathering of Muslims and non-Muslims, say *salām* to them."

The conclusion could be that if there is a mixed gathering, one could say *salām* to all of them. For example when a speaker commences with his speech in a college campus, he may greet the whole gathering with '*Assalāmu 'Ạlaykum*'.

If it is a one to one conversation and there is some benefit in saying *salām*, then there is no harm in the greeting.

If there is a possibility of harm in saying '*Assalāmu 'Ạlaykum*', e.g. it could cause a cross mix between a Muslim and non-Muslim, then it should be avoided. Once while in India, the driver who was called to drive me to Delhi was called by his Hindu name 'Sanjeet'. When he arrived and said '*Assalāmu 'Ạlaykum*', I was baffled. At first I didn't know what to say. I replied, but then I quietly enquired from someone whether he has just kept a non-Muslim name for some reason or he actually is a non-Muslim.

In reality, '*Assalāmu 'Ạlaykum*' is like a '*shi'ār*', code word for a Muslim. One *Ḥadīth* says, "Allāh gave my Ummah three gifts which He did not give to any nation before. One is '*salām*', which is the greeting of the people of *Jannah*." [73]

Therefore, one should be careful when saying *salām*. He could greet with other words like 'Hello', 'How are you?', 'Good morning' etc.

"I will ask for forgiveness for you..." Ḥaḍhrat Ibrāhīm ﷺ did ask for forgiveness for his father as mentioned in Sūrah Ibrāhīm:

رَبَّنَا اغْفِرْ لِيْ وَلِوَالِدَيَّ وَلِلْمُؤْمِنِيْنَ يَوْمَ يَقُوْمُ الْحِسَابُ ۝

"O my Lord, forgive me and my parents and all the believers, on the day when reckoning takes place." [74]

Also in Sūrah ash-Shu'arā:

وَاغْفِرْ لِأَبِيْ إِنَّهُ كَانَ مِنَ الضَّالِّيْنَ ۝

---

[73] Ḥakīm Tirmīdhī.

[74] Qur'ān 14:41.

"And forgive my father, he has been of those who went astray." [75]

However, when Ibrāhīm realised the displeasure of Allāh with his father or when his father died with *kufr*, and it was revealed to him that he has been an adversary to Allāh, Ibrāhīm stopped immediately. In Sūrah Taubah, we read:

وَمَا كَانَ اسْتِغْفَارُ اِبْرٰهِيْمَ لِاَبِيْهِ اِلَّا عَنْ مَّوْعِدَةٍ وَّعَدَهَا اِيَّاهُ ج

فَلَمَّا تَبَيَّنَ لَهٗ اَنَّهٗ عَدُوٌّ لِّلّٰهِ تَبَرَّاَ مِنْهُ ط اِنَّ اِبْرٰهِيْمَ لَاَوَّاهٌ حَلِيْمٌ ○

"And Ibrāhīm's asking for pardon for his father was only due to a promise which Ibrāhīm made to him. However, when it became clear to him that he is an enemy of God, he disowned him. Surely Ibrāhīm was of a very soft heart, forbearing." [76]

"He has been ever so kind to me..." حَفِي literally means one who receives another with extreme kindness and affection. Farrā says, "*He has full knowledge of my condition and has always been kind to me and always heard my prayers when I called Him.*"

VERSE 48

وَاَعْتَزِلُكُمْ وَمَا تَدْعُوْنَ مِنْ دُوْنِ اللّٰهِ وَاَدْعُوْ

رَبِّيْ ز عَسٰى اَلَّا اَكُوْنَ بِدُعَاءِ رَبِّيْ شَقِيًّا ﴿٤٨﴾

And I am isolating from you and all that you call upon besides Allāh, and I call upon my Lord, it is hoped that in calling my Lord I shall not be unblessed.

[75] Qur'ān 26:86.

[76] Qur'ān 9:114.

"And I am isolating from you..." 'Ạllāmah 'Ụthmānī ﷺ writes, "Ḥaḍhrat Ibrāhīm ﷺ is saying, "*When my advices have no effect on you and on the contrary you are constantly threatening me, then I have no desire to live in your town. Forsaking you and your false gods, I am migrating from this native land so that I may worship the one and only God peacefully and in seclusion. I have every hope that in worshipping Him, I will not feel deprived nor unblessed. In poverty and helplessness whenever I will call him, He will surely listen to me. My God is not a stone idol which does not hear however much you call or cry.*"

In *al-Ḥizb al-A'ẓam* we read the *du'ā*, "*O Allāh, do not make me unhappy and distressed in my calling upon you, And be extremely kind and merciful to me, O the best of those who are begged! And O the best of givers, O Most Merciful of those who show mercy.*"

Some *Mufassirīn* say that since Ibrāhīm ﷺ was leaving his family, and he himself had no children, he was saying these words hoping that Allāh ﷻ will bless him with children who can make him happy. This is why Allāh ﷻ mentions in the coming verse that We have blessed him with Is'ḥāq and Ya'qūb ﷺ and We made them both prophets as well.

VERSE 49

فَلَمَّا اعْتَزَلَهُمْ وَمَا يَعْبُدُوْنَ مِنْ دُوْنِ اللهِ لا وَهَبْنَا

لَهٗ اِسْحٰقَ وَيَعْقُوْبَ ط وَكُلًّا جَعَلْنَا نَبِيًّا ﴿٤٩﴾

Then when he had renounced them and whatever they worshipped besides Allāh, We bestowed on him Is'ḥāq and Ya'qūb, and each one We made a Prophet.

"Then when he had renounced them..." *Tafsīr Mājidī* states, "*He departed from his ancestral home in Chaldea to Syria and thence to Palestine.*" [77]

[77] Vol 3, Pg. 84.

"We bestowed on him Is'ḥāq and Ya'qūb...." 'Allāmah 'Uthmānī ﷫ writes, "Ḥaḍrat Ismā'īl ﵊ is not mentioned because he did not live with Ismā'īl ﵊. He was left with his mother in his very childhood. Moreover, Ḥaḍrat Ismā'īl ﵊ is mentioned separately in the oncoming verses."

It should be noted here that Ḥaḍrat Is'ḥāq ﵊ is the son of Ḥaḍrat Ibrāhīm ﵊. And Ḥaḍrat Ya'qub ﵊ is the son of Ḥaḍrat Is'ḥāq ﵊. Allāh ﷻ gifted Ibrāhīm ﵊ with a son as well as a grandson who grew up to be a man during his lifetime. The Hebrew name of Ya'qūb ﵊ is *Isrā'īl*. He is the ancestor of the *Banī Isrā'īl* and hundreds of prophets were raised among the *Banī Isrā'īl*.

Verse 50

وَوَهَبْنَا لَهُمْ مِّنْ رَّحْمَتِنَا وَجَعَلْنَا لَهُمْ لِسَانَ صِدْقٍ عَلِيًّا ﴿٥٠﴾

And we bestowed on them of Our mercy, and We granted them lofty honour on the tongue of truth.

"And We bestowed upon them Our mercy..." i.e. gifts both material and spiritual.[78]

'Allāmah 'Uthmānī ﷫ writes, "We gave them a great share of our special mercy. They were renowned in the world and they have been mentioned with goodness at all times throughout history. All heavenly religions and religious people hold them in high esteem. *Ummat-e-Muḥammadiyyah* remember them in *Ṣalāh* in the form of *Durūd* as an everlasting feature.

"O Allāh! ﷻ Send mercy and peace upon Muḥammad and his followers as you sent mercy and peace upon Ibrāhīm and his family. No doubt you are the All-Praised, the All-Great."

In fact, this is the result of a *du'ā* of Ḥaḍrat Ibrāhīm ﵊ which was accepted. He had prayed:

وَاجْعَل لِّي لِسَانَ صِدْقٍ فِي الْآخِرِينَ ۞

---

[78] Mājidī.

"And assign me an honourable mention among the latest generations." [79]

"And We granted them..." A.Y. Ali writes, "Abraham ﵇ and his son and grandson, Isaac and Jacob عليهما السلام, and their line maintained the banner of Allāh's ﷻ truth for many generations, and they won deservedly high praise – the praise of truth – on the tongues of men. Abraham ﵇ prayed that he should be praised by the tongue of truth among men to come in later ages. Ordinary praise may mean nothing: It may be due to selfish flattery on the part of others or artful management by the person praised. Praise on the tongue of sincere truth is praise indeed!" [80]

Verses 51-53

وَاذْكُرْ فِي الْكِتٰبِ مُوْسٰى ۚ إِنَّهُ كَانَ مُخْلَصًا وَّكَانَ رَسُوْلًا نَّبِيًّا ﴿٥١﴾ وَنَادَيْنٰهُ
مِنْ جَانِبِ الطُّوْرِ الْاَيْمَنِ وَقَرَّبْنٰهُ نَجِيًّا ﴿٥٢﴾ وَوَهَبْنَا لَهُ مِنْ رَّحْمَتِنَا اَخَاهُ
هٰرُوْنَ نَبِيًّا ﴿٥٣﴾

And mention Mūsā in the book; for He was specially chosen, he was a messenger and a prophet. We called him from the right side of Mount Ṭūr, and We drew him near, to converse in secret. And We bestowed on him, out of Our mercy, his brother Hārūn a prophet.

This is the fourth story that is being narrated. After *Khalīlullāh* (the friend of Allāh ﷻ), *Kalīmullāh* (the one with whom Allāh ﷻ spoke) is being mentioned. This may be because through the story of Ibrāhīm *Khalīlullāh* ﵇; the *Mushrikīn* of Makkah were admonished and now the attention is towards the reformation of the Jews. They are being told how much respect we have for the Prophet Mūsā ﵇; we believe that he was a prophet of great magnitude.

---

[79] Qur'ān 26:84.

[80] Pg. 865.

He was sent for the reformation of the Jews and for their emancipation from the slavery of Pharaoh.

Five qualities of Ḥaḍhrat Mūsā ﵇ are mentioned here:

[1] He was a specially chosen person. In Sūrah al-Aa'rāf, Allāh ﷻ says:

قَالَ يٰمُوْسٰىٓ اِنِّى اصْطَفَيْتُكَ عَلَى النَّاسِ بِرِسٰلٰتِيْ وَبِكَلَامِيْ ۖ
فَخُذْ مَآ اٰتَيْتُكَ وَكُنْ مِّنَ الشّٰكِرِيْنَ ۝

"He (Allāh) said O Mūsā! I have chosen you above men by my message and by my conversation (with you) so take what I have given you, and be among those who are grateful." [81]

Another qirā'ah (recital) for the word مُخْلَصًا is with 'kasrah'. i.e. '*Mukhliṣan*' (مُخْلِصًا). This means '*sincere*' person. Surely Mūsā ﵇ was an extremely sincere person. Whatever he did was for seeking the pleasure of Allāh ﷻ. In other words, he had both attributes. He was specially chosen and he was extremely sincere.

[2] He was a *Rasūl* and a *Nabī*.

A question arises here as to whether there is any difference between a *Rasūl* and a *Nabī*. The Mu'tazilah say they are both the same. *Ahl as-Sunnah* are of the opinion that the term *Nabī* is more general whereas the term *Rasūl* is more specific.

Nabī is that blessed person who receives special revelation from Allāh ﷻ. It does not matter whether he is commanded to propagate or not. A *Nabī* normally follows a *Rasūl*, either during the *Rasūl's* life or after his death. Hārūn ﵇ is a *Nabī* because he was following the *Sharīạ* of Mūsā ﵇.

[81] Qur'ān 7:144.

Similarly, Yūsha' ibn Nūn ﷺ who was the successor of Mūsā ﷺ was also a *Nabī.*

A *Rasūl* is of a higher degree. He is either a recipient of a new book or he is a legislator and brings a new *Sharīạ* or is given the orders to change some commands of the previous *Sharīạ*. He is gifted with special miracles and is commanded to combat those who refuse to accept.

Therefore, every *Rasūl* is a *Nabī*, but not every *Nabī* is a *Rasūl.*

One *Ḥadīth* in *Musnad Aḥmad* narrated by Abū Dhar al-Ghifārī ﷺ explains this. Abū Dhar ﷺ asked: "*Yā Rasūlullāh*! What is the complete number of the prophets?" He replied, "One hundred and twenty-four thousand, a huge amount." I asked, "How many *Rasūls* were amongst them?" He said, "Three hundred and thirteen." The chain of this *Ḥadīth* is weak. However, it gives indication to the vast amount of prophets Allāh ﷻ sent for the guidance of people.

Maybe this is why the Prophet ﷺ said:

> "I am the seal of prophets; there is no prophet after me (i.e. no new prophet)."

He used the word '*Nabī*' because if he had used '*Rasūl*', someone could have said that I am not a *Rasūl*, I am just a *Nabī* following Muḥammad ﷺ.

Mirza Ghulam Ahmed Qadiani attempted to deceive people in this manner when he claimed that I am a '*Ẓilli Nabī*', meaning the shadow of his Prophethood has come over me and therefore I am a prophet following Muhammad ﷺ. *Alḥamdulillāh*, the Ummah did not fall for his trap and refuted his claims with clear proofs from the Qur'ān and *Ḥadīth.*

[3] The third attribute of Mūsā ﷺ mentioned here is that Allāh ﷻ called out to him directly. This is mentioned with great detail in Sūrah al-Aa'rāf and Sūrah Ṭā-Hā.

Inshā'-Allāh, if Allāh ﷻ gives us the *tawfiq*, we will write its tafsīr and explain it there.

In short, Mūsā ﷺ was returning from Madyan after nearly ten years of absence from Egypt. His wife who was expecting their first child was with him. It was a chilly winter night when they lost their way and were wandering around the mountains and valleys of *Sīna* (Sinai). They were tired, needed some fire to warm themselves, and to use as a light. Mūsā ﷺ saw some light at a distance on a hilltop. He told his wife to wait while he would go there and bring for them a brand of fire or find a guide near the fire. He climbed the mountain and to his amazement, he saw a fire burning around a tree while the tree was intact. There was no human being there and the more the fire burnt, the more the tree shone. Mūsā ﷺ was taken aback. Suddenly, a voice from the unseen called out. This voice was coming from all sides and Mūsā ﷺ could perceive it with his whole body. "I am your Lord! Take off your shoes, you are at the sacred valley of *Ṭuwā*. I have chosen you! Therefore, listen carefully to what is being revealed. Verily I, it is I who is Allāh. There is no Deity besides me, so worship me and establish prayer for my remembrance. Verily, the hour is coming, I want to conceal it, so that each soul could be repaid for what it had earned. So do not let those people hinder you from it, who do not believe in it and who follow their whimsical desires, otherwise you will be doomed."

The conversation between Allāh ﷻ and Mūsā ﷺ goes on – if you are curious then kindly refer to Sūrah Ṭā-Hā. [82]

This is the first time Allāh ﷻ spoke to him. He again spoke to him when he came for seclusion for forty days and then was gifted with the Torah.

[4] The fourth attribute is that Allāh ﷻ made Mūsā ﷺ His '*Muqarrab*'- drew him closer to Himself. '*Muqarrabīn*' are special servants of Allāh ﷻ. Allāh ﷻ has special love for them and brings them closer to Himself, while others

[82] Qur'ān 20:9-36.

work hard to get closer to Allāh ﷻ by excessive worship and abundance of *Dhikr*. Both are good, however, the first category is of a loftier rank.

[5] The fifth attribute is mentioned with some detail in Sūrah Ṭā-Hā, where Mūsā ؑ asks Allāh ﷻ to open his heart, make easy his task, remove a certain stuttering from his tongue so that people may understand his speech, and finally to appoint his brother Hārūn ؑ as his aid who could carry his workload and support him. They would both glorify and praise Allāh ﷻ collectively and preach the message to Pharaoh and the Egyptians – Allāh ﷻ accepted his *Du'ā* and immediately gifted Hārūn ؑ with *Nubūwwah* (Prophethood).

VERSES 54-55

وَاذْكُرْ فِى الْكِتٰبِ اِسْمٰعِيْلَ ز اِنَّهٗ كَانَ صَادِقَ الْوَعْدِ

وَكَانَ رَسُوْلًا نَّبِيًّا ﴿٥٤﴾ وَكَانَ يَاْمُرُ اَهْلَهٗ بِالصَّلٰوةِ

وَالزَّكٰوةِ ص وَكَانَ عِنْدَ رَبِّهٖ مَرْضِيًّا ﴿٥٥﴾

And mention in the book Ismā'īl; he was (strictly) true to what he promised, And he was a messenger, a prophet. And He used to bid his household to Ṣalāh and Zakāh, and he was highly acceptable in the sight of his Lord.

This is the fifth story of Sayyidunā Ismā'īl ؑ. He was the eldest son of Sayyidunā Ibrāhīm ؑ and the great grandfather of the Arabs of Hijāz. He held an exclusive rank in his love of Allāh ﷻ and devotion to Him.

He is mentioned here because the Arabs used to boast over their connection to Ismā'īl ؑ. They believed that he was a great prophet of God. Therefore, Allāh ﷻ is saying that why then are they amazed at you being our prophet. Why do they say, "How is it that Allāh sent a human being as a

Prophet?" Their objection and refusal to accept is nothing but blatant rejection or ignorance.

Four characteristics of Ismā'īl ﷺ are mentioned here:

[1] True to what he promised.

[2] *Rasūl* and *Nabī*.

[3] He would command his family to establish *Ṣalāh* and give *Zakāh*.

[4] He was one with whom Allāh ﷻ was extremely pleased.

With regards to the first attribute, three narrations are narrated here:

[1] Ibn Jarīr ﷺ narrates from Sahl ibn 'Uqail ﷺ that Ismā'īl ﷺ promised one person to meet him at a certain place. He arrived on time but the man forgot. Ismā'īl ﷺ spent the whole day waiting for him. He stayed there throughout the night as well. The man appeared on the next day saying he had forgotten the promise. Ismā'īl ﷺ said, "However, I did not forget and I have been waiting for you since yesterday and I would have remained here until you arrived." In some narrations, it is said he waited for three days. Zamaksharī ﷺ narrated from Ibn 'Ạbbās ﷺ that he waited for one year.

A similar incident is narrated regarding our beloved Prophet ﷺ. Abū Dāwūd ﷺ narrates from 'Ạbdullāh ibn Abil-Hamsa ﷺ, "I struck a deal with *Rasūlullāh* ﷺ (before he became a prophet). Some remainder was left in the price of purchase. I told him to wait there and I will bring it. He agreed. I went home and completely forgot. I came back after three days and he was still waiting for me. All he said was, "*Young man, you put me in hardship, I have been waiting here for three days.*"

[2] Ibn Kathīr ﷦ narrates from Ibn Juraij ﷦ that whenever Ismā'īl ﷦ made a promise to Allāh ﷻ, he fulfilled it, meaning whenever he made a vow, he would honour it. Today people make vows and they forget or neglect them. The Qur'ān says:

$$\text{وَلْيُوْفُوْا نُذُوْرَهُمْ} \bigcirc$$

"And let them fulfil their vows." [83]

And,

$$\text{يُوْفُوْنَ بِالنَّذْرِ} \bigcirc$$

"They fulfil their vows." [84]

The Ḥadīth says:

"Whosoever vowed to obey Allāh, should obey him. And whosoever vowed to disobey Allāh should not disobey him." [85]

[3] Ismā'īl ﷦ promised his father that he would be patient at the time of being slaughtered. He said:

$$\text{سَتَجِدُنِيْ اِنْ شَاءَ اللهُ مِنَ الصّٰبِرِيْنَ} \bigcirc$$

"Allāh willing, soon you will find me from those who are patient." [86]

He kept his word and went along with his father to the place of sacrifice and lay down to be sacrificed.

Note: Keeping a promise is a noble act and a quality of a *Mu'min*. A Ḥadīth says, "When a believer makes a promise, he keeps it."

---

[83] Qur'ān 22:29.
[84] Qur'ān 76:7.
[85] Mishkāt.
[86] Qur'ān 37:102.

The Prophet ﷺ praised Abūl-'Āṣ ibn Rabī', his son in law, when he said, "He spoke to me and told me the truth and he made me a promise and kept his word."

On the other hand, breaking a promise is the habit of a hypocrite.

The Prophet ﷺ says:

> "The signs of a hypocrite are three: (i) When he speaks, he lies. (ii) When he promises, he breaks it. (iii) And when he is trusted, he betrays the trust."

[2] Ismā'īl's عليه السلام second attribute is that he was a *Rasūl* and a *Nabī*. Ibn Kathīr رحمه الله says, "This shows the preference of Ismā'īl عليه السلام over his brother Is'ḥāq عليه السلام. Because in the afore-mentioned verse, Allāh ﷻ said, "We made Is'ḥāq a *Nabī*," whereas regarding Ismā'īl, He says, "He was a *Rasūl* and a *Nabī*." In *Ṣaḥīḥ Muslim*, the Prophet ﷺ says: "Allāh chose Ismā'īl from the sons of Ibrāhīm."

Also, Is'ḥāq عليه السلام was mentioned along with his father, whereas Ismā'īl عليه السلام is mentioned separately.

Note: Some 'Ulamā say that Ismā'īl عليه السلام did not have a separate *Sharīạ*. He followed the *Sharīạ* of Ibrāhīm عليه السلام.

Tafsīr Muwāhib Ar-Raḥmān states that Ismā'īl عليه السلام was sent to the tribe of *Jurhum*. He was given some special orders with regards to that region. For example, facing the Holy Ka'bah in prayer, *Ṭawāf*, *Ḥajj*, and some *masā'il* (injunctions) regarding hunting, because that region was not a region of farming but rather they survived on hunting animals. So it seemed that Ismā'īl عليه السلام was given some special *masā'il* which were not given to Is'ḥāq عليه السلام. Therefore, Ismā'īl عليه السلام is regarded as a *Nabī* and a *Rasūl*.

[3] His third attribute is that he commanded his family to pray *Ṣalāh* and give *Zakāh*. *Ṣalāh* is the '*Ibādah* (worship) of the body, the coolness of the eyes, and brings a person closer to his Lord. *Zakāh* is the '*Ibādah* of wealth. It purifies the wealth, cures greed, and it has also been a form of worship of previous prophets.

The verse indicates that a person should begin by reforming his household.

In Sūrah Ṭā-Hā, we read:

$$\text{وَأْمُرْ اَهْلَكَ بِالصَّلٰوةِ وَاصْطَبِرْ عَلَيْهَا ۝}$$

"*Command your family to pray Ṣalāh and be steadfast upon it.*" [87]

In Sūrah At-Taḥrīm, Allāh ﷻ says:

$$\text{يَاَيُّهَا الَّذِيْنَ اٰمَنُوْٓا قُوْٓا اَنْفُسَكُمْ وَاَهْلِيْكُمْ نَارًا ۝}$$

"*O you who believe! Protect yourselves and your family from the fire.*" [88]

Allāh ﷻ also says:

$$\text{وَاَنْذِرْ عَشِيْرَتَكَ الْاَقْرَبِيْنَ ۝}$$

"*And warn your close relatives.*" [89]

Imām Abū Dāwūd ﷧ narrates from Abū Hurayrah ﷺ that the Prophet ﷺ said, "May Allāh have mercy on that man who gets up at night, then prays and awakens his wife, then if she refuses, he sprinkles water on her face. May Allāh have mercy on that woman that wakes up at night and prays, then wakes up her husband. If he refuses, she sprinkles some water in his face.'

Abū Dāwūd ﷧ narrates from Abū Saʿīd ﷺ that the Prophet ﷺ said, "When a person wakes up at night, and awakens his wife, then they both pray two *rakʿah* Ṣalāh, Allāh notes them down among those men and women who remember Allāh abundantly.'

Looking after family is extremely important, especially in this day and age. One Ḥadīth describes guardians as 'Shepherds'. This is an indication, that just as a shepherd has to be alert and careful with his herd, he has to protect them from wolves and wild beasts, similarly, a guardian should show the same care and concern for his family. We tend to neglect children, giving

---

[87] Qurʾān 20:132.

[88] Qurʾān 66:6.

[89] Qurʾān 26:214.

them total freedom, saying they will learn by their own mistakes. This attitude is wrong. We shouldn't wait for them to make mistakes. We should teach them, sit down with them and explain to them what is right and what is wrong. Otherwise, we will be throwing them into an ocean of godlessness wherein they will drown, and in the end, we will be left to cry upon our own mistakes.

May Allāh ﷻ give us the understanding to nurture our children to the best of our ability. *Āmīn.*

[4] Ismā'īl's ﷺ fourth attribute is that he was highly acceptable in the sight of his Lord. This means, he was rightly guided and he possessed excellent qualities which were pleasing to Allāh ﷻ. Thus Allāh ﷻ accepted him for sacrifice.

Tafsīr-e-Mājidī states, "He was not a rejected one, as his traducers, the Jews and the Christians would have it."

Verses 56-57

وَاذْكُرْ فِى الْكِتٰبِ اِدْرِيْسَ ز اِنَّهٗ كَانَ صِدِّيْقًا نَّبِيًّا ﴿٥٦﴾

وَرَفَعْنٰهُ مَكَانًا عَلِيًّا ﴿٥٧﴾

And mention in the Book Idrīs: He was a man of truth, a prophet. And we raised him to a lofty position.

"*And mention in the Book Idrīs...*" This is the sixth story among the stories of the prophets. Ḥadhrat Idrīs ﷺ was the grandson of Ādam ﷺ and the grandfather of Nūh ﷺ. *Tafsīr Mawāhib Ar-Raḥmān* states that he is Idrīs, son of Shīth, son of Ādam ﷺ. And Nūḥ is son of Manūshlakh, son of Idrīs ﷺ. His real name is said to be Akhnūk (Enoch). Idrīs is his title. The root of this word is '*Dars*' i.e. lesson. He was given thirty tablets by Allāh ﷻ. He used to read them and teach them. According to Jewish traditions, he was the first author and the inventor of letters, arithmetic, and astronomy. He was the first person to write with the pen and sew clothes. Scales, measurements, and weapons are also his inventions. Before his time, people used to wear animal skin.

Here, Allāh ﷻ mentions three attributes. In Sūrah al-Ambiyā, he is also regarded among the *Ṣābirīn* (the patient ones):

[1] *"He was a man of truth..."* *Tafsīr Mājidī* states, "This is perhaps to refute the opinion held by a section of the Jews that Enoch was 'inconsistent in his piety' [90], or that he was light minded and inclined to sin again." (*Na'ūdhu billāh*)

[2] *"A prophet..."* Our beloved Prophet ﷺ was taken high above the heavens for *Mi'rāj*. There he met many prophets. He met Idrīs ﷺ on the fourth heaven. [91]

[3] *"We raised him..."* There are two interpretations with regards to this, 'raising to a lofty position':

[i] This raising is spiritual i.e. he held a lofty status in the eyes of Allāh ﷻ. Ibn 'Abbās ؓ says, "Idrīs ﷺ was a tailor. Whenever he would sew a cloth and pierce the needle, he would say '*SubḥānAllāh*'. Thus by nightfall, there would be no one with more virtuous deeds than him."

Allāh ﷻ says regarding our Prophet ﷺ: وَرَفَعْنَا لَكَ ذِكْرَكَ - '*And we have raised for you your name.*'

[ii] This raising is in a physical form. Ibn Kathīr ؓ narrates from Mujāhid ؓ, "*Idrīs ﷺ did not die, he was raised just as 'Īsā ﷺ was raised.*" Muwāhib Ar-

---

> Raḥmān رحمه الله narrates from some *Mufassirīn* who say that four prophets are still alive, two in the earth: Khadhir and Ilyās عليهما السلام, and two in the sky: 'Īsā and Idrīs عليهما السلام.

Ḥasan Baṣrī رحمه الله says, "He was raised to *Jannah.*" *Tafsīr Ma'ālim at-Tanzīl* relates the following passage from ibn Wahb رحمه الله:

"During the time of Idrīs عليه السلام, when people's *A'māl* (deeds) were taken to Allāh ﷻ, his were the most every day. The angels were amazed at his high level of servitude, love and devotion. The Angel of Death felt this urge to visit him and sought permission from the Almighty which was granted. He came to Idrīs عليه السلام and saw him fasting every day. At *ifṭār* time, he offered food to *Malak al-Maut* (the Angel of Death), not knowing who he was. He refused. On the second day, he refused again and on the third day he refused again. Thereupon, Idrīs عليه السلام asked him, "Who are you?" He replied, "I am *Malak al-Maut.* I took permission from Allāh ﷻ to visit you."

Idrīs عليه السلام asked him, "Will you do me a favour by extracting my soul and then returning it?" He agreed and after seeking permission from Allāh ﷻ, he did so. Then *Malak al-Maut* asked him, "Why did you do this?" He replied, "So that I can understand the pangs of death and be prepared for it when it comes."

Then he asked for another favour; to take him to the heavens so that he could see *Jannah* and *Jahannam.* Allāh ﷻ gave permission and *Malak al-Maut* took him into the heavens. When they came near hell, Idrīs عليه السلام said, "Can I go inside and greet Mālik (its caretaker)?" This was done. Thereafter, he said, "You have shown me *Jahannam*, now show me *Jannah* as well." *Malak al-Maut* took him inside *Jannah.* Idrīs عليه السلام was roaming around enjoying its luxuries. *Malak al-Maut* said, "Come on now, we have to go, so that I can take you back to your place." Idrīs عليه السلام grabbed hold of one tree and said, "I am not leaving this place."

Allāh ﷻ then sent an angel to judge between them. He asked Idrīs عليه السلام, "Why are you not going out of here?" He replied, "Because Allāh ﷻ has said, 'Every soul shall taste death' and I have tasted it. He has said, 'Every person has to come to *Jahannam*', and I have been to it. And Allāh ﷻ has said, 'They will not be driven out of *Jannah*', so I am not going out of here." Then Allāh ﷻ said to *Malak al-Maut*, "With my permission he arrived, and with my permission he will stay here. Leave him." Thus Idrīs عليه السلام is now alive in *Jannah*.'

Wahb ibn Munabbih رحمه الله says, "Therefore Idrīs عليه السلام is now in *Jannah*, sometimes eating its fruits and other times worshipping Allāh ﷻ with the angels." [92]

There are other narrations as well regarding his befriending the angel of the sun and asking him to take him to the rising place of the sun. We have left them due to fear of the book becoming too lengthy, and due to the fact that Imām Ibn Kathīr رحمه الله has criticised these narrations.

Tafsīr Mājidī states here that this lofty position may be a place as well as a position. So the words of the Holy Qur'ān do not necessarily support the Jewish and the Christian view that Enoch was raised alive to heaven.

The Bible and its commentaries relate, 'And he was not; for God took him.' [93] 'The meaning of the expression 'he was not; for God took him,' is no doubt, correctly given by the writer of Heb, as that Enoch never died, but he was translated to heaven, like Elijah, as a reward for the holiness of his life. [94] 'By faith Enoch was translated that he should not see death; and was not found, because God 'had translated him!' [95] 'Enoch was a pious worshipper of the true God, and was removed from among the dwellers on earth to heaven. Enoch is one of those that passed into Garden of Eden without tasting the pangs of death.' [96] [97]

Verse 58

أُولَٰئِكَ الَّذِينَ أَنْعَمَ اللَّهُ عَلَيْهِم مِّنَ النَّبِيِّينَ مِن ذُرِّيَّةِ آدَمَ ۚ وَمِمَّنْ

---

[92] Tafsīr Qurṭubī, Vol 11, Pg. 119.

[93] Ge. 5:24.

[94] Dummelow, op. cit. Pg. 13.

[95] He. 11:5.

[96] JE. V. Pg. 178.

[97] Para 184, Vol 3, Pg. 87.

حَمَلْنَا نُوحٍ ز وَّمِنْ ذُرِّيَّةِ اِبْرٰهِيْمَ وَاِسْرَآءِيْلَ وَمِمَّنْ هَدَيْنَا وَاجْتَبَيْنَا ط
اِذَا تُتْلٰى عَلَيْهِمْ اٰيٰتُ الرَّحْمٰنِ خَرُّوْا سُجَّدًا وَّبُكِيًّا ﴿٥٨﴾

These are the people whom Allāh has blessed with bounties, the prophets from the progeny of Ādam, and of those whom We caused to board (the Ark) with Nūḥ, and from the progeny of Ibrāhīm and Isrā'īl (Jacob) and from those whom We guided and selected. When the verses of the Ar-Raḥmān (the compassionate) were recited before them, they used to fall down in sajdah (prostration), weeping.

From the beginning of the *sūrah*, special attributes of specific prophets have been mentioned. Now Allāh ﷻ is mentioning a general attribute of all the prophets: the quality of being extremely humble and submissive to the commands of Allāh ﷻ. Allāh ﷻ chose them, guided them, and blessed them with special bounties. In spite of such a high status, they remained engaged in devotion and whenever they used to hear the verses of Allāh ﷻ, they would fall into prostration (*sajdah*) and cry in front of Allāh ﷻ. The purpose of mentioning this is to urge us to follow them, and to stay well away from the path of neglectful people.

Ibn Jarīr رحمه الله says, "*From the children of Ādam...*" refers to Idrīs عليه السلام. "*From those who we carried with Nūḥ...*" is indicating to Ibrāhīm عليه السلام. "*From the progeny of Ibrāhīm...*" refers to Is'ḥāq, Ya'qub, and Ismā'īl عليهم السلام. And "*...from the progeny of Isrā'īl (Ya'qūb)*" refers to Mūsā, Hārūn, Zakarīyyā, Yaḥyā, and 'Īsā عليهم السلام (son of Maryam عليها السلام)."

"*From whom we guided and selected...*" Allāh ﷻ gave them guidance to the straight path and chose them for the designation of Prophethood and Messengership. [98]

Qurṭubī رحمه الله says, "We guided them towards Islam and chose them for *Īmān*."

---

[98] 'Uthmānī, Pg. 1937.

"When verses of Ar-Raḥmān are recited..." The verse indicates that when a person hears the words of Allāh ﷻ, he should feel their effects in his heart.

The *Ḥadīth* says:

"The Qur'ān was revealed with sorrow, so read it with sadness, and when you read it, cry. If you cannot cry, then make the face of someone who is crying." [99]

The Prophet ﷺ and the *Ṣaḥābah* used to cry whilst reading the Qur'ān in *Tahajjud Ṣalāh*. 'Umar ibn Khaṭṭāb ؓ recited this verse and fell into sajdah, then he said, "This is the sajdah but where is the weeping." – Meaning how can we weep like the prophets? Ibn 'Abbās ؓ says, "When you recite a verse of *sajdah*, do not hasten in performing sajdah until you cry a little, if your eyes cannot cry, let your heart weep."

One *Ḥadīth* says:

"The fire of *Jahannam* will not touch two eyes; one which wept due to the fear of Allāh and the other which stayed awake at night (to ensure the security of the army) in the path of Allāh."

In *Ṣaḥīḥ Bukhārī*, it is narrated that Abū Bakr as-Ṣiddīq ؓ used to cry profusely whilst reciting the Qur'ān.

Ṣāliḥ al-Murrī saw the Prophet ﷺ in a dream and recited some Qur'ān to him. The Prophet ﷺ said, "This is reciting but where is the crying?" It is said that after this incident, he would cry so much that he would make the gathering weep. Imām Nawawī ؒ states in his commentary of *Ṣaḥīḥ Muslim*, "Some people passed away in his gathering after hearing his recitation."

The aim is to ponder over the verses, to think about our beginning and ending, and the standing before Allāh ﷻ thereby softening the heart. Once

[99] Ibn Mājah.

the heart is soft, it will attract the 'Raḥmah' (mercy) of Allāh ﷻ thereby resulting in weeping.

Ibn al-'Arabī ﵁ says, "The prophets used to listen to the words of the Qur'ān with their ears, and ponder over its meanings with their hearts, and with their souls they would rise to the highest positions where they would observe the manifestations of the speaker (i.e. Allāh) which would cause them to fall into prostration and weep."

<u>Note</u>: Upon reciting this verse, *sajdah* becomes *Wājib* (compulsory) according to the madhab of Imām Abū Ḥanīfah ﵀.

VERSE 59

$$فَخَلَفَ مِنْ بَعْدِهِمْ خَلْفٌ اَضَاعُوا الصَّلٰوةَ$$

$$وَاتَّبَعُوا الشَّهَوٰتِ فَسَوْفَ يَلْقَوْنَ غَيًّا ﴿٥٩﴾$$

Then there came after them such successors who neglected Ṣalāh and followed (their selfish) desires. So they will soon face (the outcome of their) deviation.

"Then came after them..." In the previous verses, Allāh ﷻ mentioned the group of fortunate people i.e. the prophets and those followers who respected the limits set by Allāh ﷻ, who held on to the commands of Allāh ﷻ, who practiced on His orders and refrained from His prohibitions.

Now Allāh ﷻ is mentioning those evil minded people who came after them and neglected all commands of Allāh ﷻ. They abandoned such an important aspect of *Dīn* as *Ṣalāh*. Thus, such people were doomed and they shall face the consequences, except for those who repent from their life of sinning, and turn towards Allāh ﷻ. Such people's *Tawbah* will be accepted and they will be joined to the first group.

This comparison is to show us that success lies in following the commands of Allāh ﷻ as shown by the prophets whereas the root of destruction is in its neglect, turning away, heedlessness and following lusts and whimsical desires.

"*Who neglected Ṣalāh . . .*" This could have several meanings:

[1] Ibn Jarīr narrates from Suddī and Muḥammad ibn Ka'b al-Quraẓī that abandoning means leaving aside altogether. This is why Imām Aḥmad and many scholars are of the opinion that a neglecter of *Ṣalāh* becomes a *Kāfir*. They put forward the *Ḥadīth*, "*Between a man and shirk is leaving Ṣalāh.*" i.e. one who doesn't perform *Ṣalāh* has entered the fold of *Shirk.* [100]

Another *Ḥadīth* says, "The distinction between us and them is *Ṣalāh*, so whosoever leaves it has committed *Kufr* (disbelief)."

[2] Imām Awza'ī says, "Neglecting means praying out of time because if they would have left it altogether they would have become *Kāfirs*."

Ibn Mas'ūd was asked, "Allāh very frequently mentions *Ṣalāh* in the Qur'ān: "...who are punctual of *Ṣalāh*..." "...who are constant readers of *Ṣalāh*..." etc. Ibn Mas'ūd said, "This means to pray at the right time.' Masrūq says, "Whosoever is punctual of five daily *Ṣalāh* will not be included with those who are neglectful. In leaving them is destruction. Leaving means not praying on time."

Once 'Umar ibn 'Abd al-Azīz recited the above verse, "There came after them a generation who abandoned *Ṣalāh*..." Then he said, "Their abandoning was not leaving prayer altogether but rather, it was their neglect of the appropriate times."

Mujāhid said, "This will happen closer to the Doomsday. The pious ones will have left this world, the evil ones will be jumping over one another in the streets." In another narration he says, "They in this Ummah will be those who will ride over one another in the streets just as cattle and donkeys do so, they will not fear Allāh above nor will they be ashamed of people in the earth."

[100] Muslim, Abū Dāwūd, Tirmīdhī.

How many people do we see today neglecting *Ṣalāh* altogether? Many pray but are not careful of the times. During the summer months, people set their alarm clocks at the time of going for work. They deliberately neglect their Fajr *Ṣalāh*. Some might pray *Qaḍā'* at eight o'clock before going for work, but this is an intentional *Qaḍā'*.

We used to hear the story of a girl that died. When her brother returned after burial, he realised that during the burial some valuables had fallen out of his pockets and into the grave. He went back and opened the grave. For a few moments he saw an alarming scene. He saw that his sister was being punished in fire. He returned home and enquired from his mother whether the deceased had been involved in some major sins. She replied, "*All I can remember is that she used to feel that Ṣalāh was a burden and would often make it Qaḍā'.*" i.e. pray after the time had passed.

She at least prayed *Qaḍā'*, what will happen to those who don't pray at all? We still have time to make amends. We should give ourselves a fresh start and perform *Ṣalāh* properly. May Allāh ﷻ give us the *tawfīq* and ability. *Āmīn.*

[3] Imām Qurṭubī رحمه الله narrates from Al-Qāsim ibn Mukhaymirah and 'Ạbdullāh ibn Mas'ūd رضي الله عنه that abandoning *Ṣalāh* means not praying at appropriate times as well as not fulfilling the due rights of *Ṣalāh*.

This is so because when a *Ṣalāh* is not performed correctly, it is as though it has not been prayed at all. It is for this reason that once a *Ṣaḥābī* رضي الله عنه entered the Masjid, performed two *rak'ạh* and attended the *majlis* of *Rasūlullāh* ﷺ who told him to go back and repeat his *Ṣalāh*. His words were, "Go back and pray again because you have not prayed." The *Ṣaḥābī* رضي الله عنه did so but again *Rasūlullāh* ﷺ sent him back. This happened a third time as well. So the person said, "*Yā Rasūlullāh*! Teach me, because this is the best I can pray." Then *Rasūlullāh* ﷺ instructed him not to hasten in performing the *arkān* and to perform *rukū'*, *sujūd*, *qawma* and *jalsa* with *khushū'* (humbleness).

Sayyidunā Huzaifah رضي الله عنه saw a careless person cutting corners in his *Ṣalāh*. He asked, "How long have you been praying like this? He replied, "For forty years." Huzaifah ﷺ said, "You have never prayed. If you were to die praying like this, you would die on something other than the *Fiṭrah* of Muḥammad ﷺ" (*Fiṭrah* means natural religion; here it could mean the *Sunnah*).

One *Ḥadīth* says, "The *Ṣalāh* of such a person is not valid who does not straighten his back (in *rukū'* and *sujūd*)." Another *Ḥadīth* says, "The worst thief is he who steals in *Ṣalāh*" (i.e. one whose movements are hasty and against the *Sunnah*).

Another *Ḥadīth* says, "That is the *Ṣalāh* of a hypocrite. One who was sat in wait for the sun, until when it was between the two horns of Satan, he got up and pecked four times; he did not remember Allāh in them except a little."

Imām Qurṭubī ﷺ after narrating the above *Aḥādīth* summarises and says, "The conclusion is that one who is not careful about completing the *wuḍū'*, *rukū'*, and *sujūd* is not careful about *Ṣalāh*; one who is not careful about *Ṣalāh* has abandoned it. One who abandons *Ṣalāh* will abandon other aspects even more, just as one who is careful regarding *Ṣalāh*, will be more careful regarding other aspects of *Dīn*. There is no *Dīn* of a person who has no *Ṣalāh*."

Imām Qurṭubī ﷺ goes on to narrate some *Aḥādīth* regarding the *Ḥisāb* (reckoning and accounting) of *Ṣalāh* on the Day of Judgement. Abū Hurairah ﷺ reports that the Prophet ﷺ said, "The first account to be taken from a man on the day of *Qiyāmah* will be of *Ṣalāh*. If he has completed his *Ṣalāh* (then that is acceptable) otherwise Allāh ﷻ will say, "See whether my servant has any *Nawāfil*." Then if he does have any *Nawāfil*, the *Farā'iḍ* will be completed by them."

Qurṭubī ﷺ writes: "It is desirable for a person to perform his *Farā'iḍ* properly, and then perform some *Nawāfil* as well because *Nawāfil* will draw a person closer to his Lord." The *Ḥadīth al-Qudsī* says, "My servant constantly brings himself closer to me through *Nawāfil* until I begin to love him. Then when I love him, I become his ears by which he listens, his eyes by which he sees, and his hands by which he holds. Then if he asks me I will give him. If he seeks my refuge, I will give him protection."

Ibn 'Abd al-Barr Mālikī ﷺ says, "*Nawāfil* cannot compensate for *Farā'iḍ*. Therefore, this will only be for people who mistakenly missed a *Farḍh*, or someone who prayed *Farḍh* but without proper *rukū'* and *sujūd* - because such *Ṣalāh* is regarded as incomplete."

In this day and age, we see some people content with *Farḍh Ṣalāh* alone. They fail to perform the *Sunnah Mua'kkadah*, never mind *Nawāfil*.

A friend of mine is a teacher at a school in Jeddah. He says that at *Dhuhr* time, the teachers just pray four *Farḍh*. Nobody prays the four *Sunnah* before or the two *Sunnah* after. They would sit there and talk loudly, but would not pray the *Sunnah*. I may be the only one who performs the *Sunnah*. Once I tried explaining to someone who I took as a friend that the closeness of Allāh ﷻ can only be achieved through *Nawāfil* as it is mentioned in a *Ḥadīth* al-Qudsī. But he did not want to understand.

These people argue with the *Ḥadīth* of the Bedouin who said, "By Allāh, I will not do more or less than this" (i.e. what you have taught me about five daily *Farḍh*, the fasting of *Ramadhan*, and the payment of compulsory *Zakāh*). The Prophet ﷺ remarked, "If he is saying the truth, he will enter *Jannah*."

These people fail to understand that this Bedouin had just converted to Islam. Such people should only be taught *Farā'iḍ*. Then when they are well acquainted with *Dīn* and they themselves develop the desire to pray more, they will offer optional prayers. Besides, it is better to follow Abū Bakr and Umar ؓ and their like who never missed any *Sunnah* rather than following a Bedouin.

Regarding the *Sunnah*, there are many *Aḥādīth*:

[1] "Whosoever is punctual of twelve *rak'ah* daily, Allāh will construct a palace for him in *Jannah*." [101]

[2] "The two (*Sunnah*) *rak'ah* of *Fajr* are more beloved to me than the *Dunyā* and whatever it contains."

[101] Tirmīdhī.

[3] "Four *rak'ah* before Dhuhr are such that the doors of heaven are opened upon them."

[4] "Whosoever prays six *rak'ats* after *Maghrib* and does not speak any evil in between, that [worship] will be equal to the worship of twelve years." [102]

Abul 'Ạbbās al-Qurṭubī ﷫ has stated in his commentary on *Ṣaḥīḥ Muslim* that one who continuously and habitually leaves the *Sunnah Mua'kkadah* is a *Fāsiq* (flagrant sinner). This is because *Rasūlullāh* ﷺ said, "*Whosoever turns away from my Sunnah is not from me (i.e. is not a follower of my ways).*" So the least these words can indicate is *fisq*. He also writes that the *Ṣaḥābah*, *Tābi'īn* and our *Salaf* never made any distinction between *Farā'iḍ* and *Nawāfil*. They performed everything with punctuality. Maybe they were more punctual about their *Nawāfil* than we are about our *Farā'iḍ*. It was the *fuqahā* (jurists) who had to separate the *Nafl* and *Sunnah* from the *Wājib* and *Farḍh*, so that an explanation could be made regarding *Qaḍā'* i.e. that for which *Qaḍā'* is necessary and that for which it is not compulsory. May Allāh ﷻ give *hidāyah* (guidance) to the whole *Ummah* and give us the *tawfīq* to practice properly. *Āmīn*.

Another important *mas'ala* which needs to be clarified here is regarding *Qaḍā-e-'Umrī*. This *mas'ala* has also emanated due to the unfortunate circumstances of the times we live in. During the golden era, people could not even think of someone having not performed prayer continuously for many years. In those times, even the *Munāfiqs* were punctual, because they feared being caught out.

Today we see people hearing the *Adhān* and yet they keep busy in their task as though nothing has happened. Some people think that *Ṣalāh* is only for old people. When you have white hair then you hold a *tasbīh* in your hand and start *Ṣalāh*. Others think only fools keep rushing to the mosque for *Ṣalāh*.

---

[102] Tirmīdhī, Ibn Mājah.

Now the *mas'ala* arises wherein a person realises his neglect. He feels guilty and repents. He wants to perform *Qaḍā'* of the missed *Ṣalāh*. Should he do so or not?

We see the minority group of Salafists who will say to such people that you have done your *tawbah* so you are now a new person, therefore you do not have to perform any *Qaḍā'*. One so called scholar declared this with great conviction on Islam Channel. The lady preacher Dr. Raf'at Hashimi also holds this opinion. They trace this back to Ibn Taymīyyah.

When we go a bit further down in history, we see that the four Imāms agree unanimously on the *mas'ala* of *Qaḍā-e-'Umrī*. Imām Aḥmad ﷺ goes to the extent that performing *Qaḍā'* with *tartīb* (order) is also *Wājib*. He says: "Whosoever missed the *Ṣalāh* of a whole year, shall perform them. He will read every *Ṣalāh* while remembering whatever *Ṣalāh* he missed out." [103]

The necessity of *Qaḍā'* being in order is narrated from 'Ạbdullāh ibn 'Umar ﷺ, Ibrāhīm an-Nakha'ī ﷺ, az-Ẓuhrī ﷺ, Rabī'ạh ﷺ, Yaḥyā al-Anṣārī ﷺ, Imām Mālik ﷺ, Layth ibn Sạ'd ﷺ, Imām Abū Ḥanīfah ﷺ, and Is'ḥāq ibn Rahwayh ﷺ. Their evidence is in the *Ḥadīth* narrated by Imām Tirmidhī ﷺ in the chapter entitled 'The Chapter in Relation to: A person who misses many *Ṣalāh* - with which should he begin?' and by Nasa'ī ﷺ in the chapter 'The Chapter in Relation to: How one should make up for the missed *Ṣalāh*.'

The Prophet ﷺ, during the Battle of *Khandaq* missed four *Ṣalāh*. He performed them in order. He commanded Bilāl ﷺ who said the *Iqāmah* then he prayed *Dhuhr*. Then he commanded him so Bilāl ﷺ said *Iqāmah* then he performed '*Aṣr*. Then he commanded him and Bilāl ﷺ said *Iqāmah*, then he performed *Maghrib*. Then he instructed him and Bilāl ﷺ said *Iqāmah* then he performed '*Ishā'*. He has taught us, "Pray as you have seen me pray." Therefore, *Qaḍā'* will be performed with order as he had done.

[1] In fact, one *Ḥadīth* narrated by Abū Yạ'lā Al Mawṣilī ﷺ says, "If a person forgot a missed *Ṣalāh*, then he did not remember it until he had started the

---

[103] Al-Mughnī, Vol. 2, Pg. 336.

next one with the *Imām*, then he should continue with the *Imām*. When he completes the *Ṣalāh*, he should read *Qaḍā'* of the *Ṣalāh* he missed, then he should repeat the *Ṣalāh* which he prayed with the Imām." The chain of this *Ḥadīth* is *Ḥasan*.

[2] However, Imām Abū Ḥanīfah ؒ and Imām Mālik ؒ are of the opinion that *tartīb* (order) is only *Wājib* if the amount of *Ṣalāh* that are missed are five or less (the *Ṣalāh* of one day). If they are more than five, then the necessity of *tartīb* will be omitted, because it will be difficult to remember the order and it could lead to repeating *Qaḍā'* all the time. *Tartīb* will be forgiven just as the *tartīb* in *Qaḍā'* of fasting is forgiven.

[3] Imām Shafi'ī ؒ is of the opinion that *tartīb* is not necessary even if the *Qaḍā' Ṣalāh* are less than five. [104]

Note: If *Qaḍā'* are plenty, then only *Farḍh* and *Witr Wājib* will have to be performed, not *Sunnah*. Therefore, one day *Qaḍā'* will be of 20 *Rak'ah*: 2 for *Fajr*, 4 for *Dhuhr*, 4 for 'Aṣr, 3 for *Maghrib*, 4 for 'Ishā and 3 *Witr*. If a *Ṣalāh* was missed during a journey and *Qaḍā'* is being done at home, *Qaṣr* will have to be done – i.e. 2 instead of 4. If there was only one *Qaḍā'*, the *Sunnah* could also be repeated. The Prophet ﷺ once missed *Fajr*. When performing *Qaḍā'*, he prayed *Sunnah* as well.

If a person was to be in the state of unconsciousness, then there are three opinions regarding *Qaḍā'* of the missed *Ṣalāh*:

[1] Imām Mālik ؒ and Imām Shafi'ī ؒ are of the opinion that he does not have to perform any *Ṣalāh* besides the one in which he woke up and had enough time to pray.

---

[104] Al Mughnī, Vol.2, Pg. 337.

[2] Imām Abū Ḥanīfah ﷺ says that if he was unconscious for less than one day, he has to perform *Qaḍā'* of the missed *Ṣalāh*. If it is for more than one day, then he does not have to do so.

[3] Imām Aḥmad ibn Ḥanbal ﷺ says that he will have to perform *Qaḍā'* for however many days he had slept. His evidence is in the incident of 'Ammār ibn Yāsir ﷺ. He fainted and came back to his senses after three days. He asked, "Have I prayed." They replied, "You have not prayed for three days." He said, "Bring me water." He then performed *wuḍū'* and performed the missed *Ṣalāh* throughout the night.

If a person is affected by madness and insanity, then he is classed as '*Majnūn*'. He will not be regarded as *Mukallaf*, therefore, *Qaḍā'* will not be necessary. If a person was intoxicated by alcohol or drugs, he will have to perform *Qaḍā'* of the missed *Ṣalāh*. The difference is that the illness of a *majnūn* is from Allāh ﷻ, whereas intoxication is a person's deliberate act. [105]

Once whilst commentating on the *Ḥadīth*, "The first account to be taken from a person on the day of *Qiyāmah* will be of *Ṣalāh*," I explained to the gathering that on one side will be the list of *Ṣalāh* that were due, and on the other side will be a list of the ones that were prayed e.g. 5 *Ṣalāh* x 365 = 1825. If a person lived for 65 years and he had reached puberty at the age of 15, then his due *Ṣalāh* will be as follows:

50 years x 1825 = 91,250 - so one must be very careful and punctual regarding *Ṣalāh* and make Qaḍā' of whatever is due. One elderly person aged 70 made a firm resolution and started *Qaḍā'* – slowly he reached up to 150 *rak'ah* everyday – Thereafter, he pushed it up to *200* and then *300* rak'ah every day. Since he was retired he would pray all day. *Alḥamdulillāh*, within three years he completed the account of his whole life. He could not control his happiness when he completed the *Qaḍā'* – He had a feeling of jubilation and satisfaction.

---

[105] These *masā'il* have been taken from Al-Mughnī, Vol. 2, Pg. 51-52.

The same rule applies to *Qaḍā'* of *Zakāh*, *Ṣawm* and *Ḥajj*. Only a non-Muslim who embraces Islam does not have to perform *Qaḍā'* of the *Ṣalāh* he missed throughout his life. Some people get mistaken and apply the same rule to a Muslim who repents after a life of sinning.

May Allāh ﷻ give us the correct understanding of *Dīn* and the ability to practice. *Āmīn.*

"And they followed their (lustful) desires..." Ibn Kathīr رحمه الله narrates from Abūl Ash-hab رحمه الله who said, "Allāh ﷻ revealed to Sayyidunā Dāwūd عليه السلام, "O Dāwūd! Warn your companions regarding eating desirable foods. Because when the hearts are attached to the desires of this *Dunyā*, the minds are curtained from me. And the least I do to a servant from my servants, when he gives preference to a desire from his desires, is that I deprive him from my obedience."

Imām Qurṭubī رحمه الله narrates from 'Alī رضي الله عنه, "It is one who builds huge mansions and rides such mounts which are connected in line, one after the other and wears clothes for fame."

'*Shahwah*' is something which is in harmony with a person, he desires it and he does not refrain from it. [106]

Rūḥ al-Ma'ānī states, "The term '*Shahwah*' includes everything that diverts a person away from *Ṣalāh* and the remembrance of Allāh ﷻ."

Bukhārī رحمه الله narrates the *Ḥadīth*, "*Jannah* is surrounded by *Makārih* (matters which are disliked) whereas *Jahannam* is surrounded by *Shahawāt* (carnal desires)."

Another *Ḥadīth* explains that when Allāh ﷻ created *Jannah*, he instructed Jibrā'īl عليه السلام to go and have a look at it. He did so and said it is possible that every single person will enter it (due to its luxuries and the pleasurable things it contains). Then Allāh ﷻ covered it with matters which are disliked and instructed Jibrā'īl عليه السلام to have a look. He had a look and returned saying, "It seems nobody will be able to enter," (due to the amount of sacrifices

[106] Qurṭubī.

people would have to make in leaving their carnal desires). Then Allāh created *Jahannam* and instructed Jibrā'īl عليه السلام to have a look. He did so and remarked that it is so terrifying, no one will enter it. Then Allāh ﷻ curtained it with *Shahawāt* (desires) and instructed him to have a look. Jibrā'īl عليه السلام returned and said I fear that everyone will enter it (because people like fulfilling their carnal desires without being careful about *Ḥalāl*, *Ḥarām*, etc.).

Ibn Kathīr رحمه الله narrates from Ka'b Al-Aḥbār who is reported to have said, "By Allāh ﷻ, I find the description of hypocrites in the book of Allāh ﷻ: drinkers of *qahwās*, neglecters of *Ṣalāh*, players with dice, sleepers from the *Ṣalāhs* of Darkness (i.e. '*Ishā* and *Fajr*), wasters of time in the morning, and abandoners of the congregation."

Ḥasan Baṣrī رحمه الله said, "They are people who emptied the *Masājid* and stuck to their properties."

"They will soon face ghayy..." غَيّ has been translated by Muftī Taqī Ṣāḥib as '(The outcome of) their deviation.' The root of the word is '*ghawāyah*', which means missing the mark.

Mufassirīn have put forward various interpretations for this word. Ibn Kathīr رحمه الله narrates, "'Ibn 'Abbās رضي الله عنه says, "They will suffer huge loss."' Qatādah رحمه الله says, "Evil." Ibn Mas'ūd رضي الله عنه says, "*Ghayy* is the name of a valley in *Jahannam* full of blood and pus."

Qurṭubī رحمه الله adds from Ibn 'Abbās رضي الله عنه who said, "*Ghayy* is a valley in *Jahannam*, even the other valleys of *Jahannam* seek protection from its heat. Allāh ﷻ has prepared that valley for the adulterer who is persistent upon adultery, the drinker who is addicted to intoxicants, the consumer of interest money who does not stop from it, and for those who hurt their parents, and for those who forge testimonies, and for a woman who brought upon her husband a child which does not belong to him (i.e. through fornication)."

May Allāh ﷻ protect us from all forms of sins and from their evil outcome. *Āmīn.*

VERSE 60

إِلَّا مَنْ تَابَ وَاٰمَنَ وَعَمِلَ صَالِحًا فَاُولٰئِكَ
يَدْخُلُوْنَ الْجَنَّةَ وَلَا يُظْلَمُوْنَ شَيْئًا ﴿٦٠﴾

Except those who repent and believe and work righteously, for they will enter Jannah (the Garden) and they will not be wronged at all.

"Except for those who repent..." Qurṭubī ﷺ says, "Who repent from abandoning *Ṣalāh* and following carnal desires and turn towards the obedience of their Lord." Ibn Kathīr ﷺ adds: "Then Allāh ﷻ will accept their repentance, will give them a good ending, and make them from among the inheritors of *Jannah*. This is because '*Tawbah*' abolishes all sins committed prior to it. A *Ḥadīth* says, "The one who repents from a sin is like one who has no sin." [107]

Maybe this is why Allāh ﷻ moves on to say, "They will not be wronged at all." This means that whatever good deed they perform after their repentance, there will be no reduction in its reward. They will not be reproached for what they had been doing before. Their previous sins had been washed away completely, and this was due to the grace of the Most Graceful and the mercy of the Most Merciful.

In Sūrah al-Furqān, Allāh ﷻ says:

إِلَّا مَنْ تَابَ وَاٰمَنَ وَعَمِلَ عَمَلًا صَالِحًا فَاُولٰئِكَ يُبَدِّلُ اللهُ
سَيِّاٰتِهِمْ حَسَنَاتٍ ؕ وَكَانَ اللهُ غَفُوْرًا رَّحِيْمًا ۝ وَمَنْ تَابَ وَعَمِلَ
صَالِحًا فَاِنَّهٗ يَتُوْبُ اِلَى اللهِ مَتَابًا ۝

"...Except for those who repent and believe and perform righteous deeds, then they are such that Allāh will turn their vices into virtues, And Allāh is All-Forgiving, Most

---

107 Ibn Mājah and Ḥakīm Tirmidhī.

Merciful... And whosoever repents and does good deeds, then surely he is turning towards Allāh in earnestness." [108]

VERSE 61

جَنّٰتِ عَدْنِ الَّتِي وَعَدَ الرَّحْمٰنُ

عِبَادَهُ بِالْغَيْبِ ۚ إِنَّهُ كَانَ وَعْدُهُ مَأْتِيًّا ﴿٦١﴾

Gardens of eternity which the Compassionate one has promised to His bondsmen, (though yet) unseen. Verily His promise is ever to be fulfilled.

"Gardens of eternity..." Allāh ﷻ is describing the type of gardens in which they will be admitted. Their first quality is eternity. In other verses, Allāh ﷻ says,

لَا يَبْغُوْنَ عَنْهَا حِوَلًا ۝

"They will never feel like moving from there." [109]

خٰلِدِيْنَ فِيْهَا اَبَدًا ۝

"They will remain in there for ever." [110]

عَطَاءً غَيْرَ مَجْذُوْذٍ ۝

"A gift which will never be cut off." [111]

اِنَّ هٰذَا لَرِزْقُنَا مَالَهٗ مِنْ نَّفَادٍ ۝

"This is our provision, for which there is no end." [112]

---

[108] Qur'ān 25:70-71.

[109] Qur'ān 18:108.

[110] Qur'ān 98:8

[111] Qur'ān 11:108.

[112] Qur'ān 38:54.

اُكُلُهَا دَآئِمٌ وَّظِلُّهَا ○

"Its food is everlasting and (so is) its shade." [113]

وَمَاهُمْ مِّنْهَا بِمُخْرَجِيْنَ ○

"They will never be driven out of there." [114]

A *Ḥadīth* in the *Ṣiḥāḥ* says, "An announcer will announce, O dwellers of *Jannah*! It has been destined for you to remain healthy forever and never fall ill, and remain young forever and never grow old, and that you live forever and never die." [115]

"Whosoever enters *Jannah* will enjoy and never grieve, his clothes will not wear out nor will his youth fade." [116]

After the slaughter of Death, the announcement will be made, "O people of *Jannah*, Eternity (is yours) therefore no death."

The second thing is that this is a promise which Allāh ﷻ has made to his servants, and who fulfils their promise better than Allāh ﷻ? In Sūrah Taubah, we read:

وَعْدًا عَلَيْهِ حَقًّا فِى التَّوْرٰيةِ وَالْاِنْجِيْلِ
وَالْقُرْاٰنِ ط وَمَنْ اَوْفٰى بِعَهْدِهٖ مِنَ اللّٰهِ ○

"(*This is*) *A promise which is due upon Him,* (*mentioned*) *in the Torah, Bible, and the Qur'ān. And who could be more faithful to his covenant than Allāh?*" [117]

In Sūrah an-Nisā, Allāh ﷻ says,

---

[113] Qur'ān 13:35.

[114] Qur'ān 15:48.

[115] Muslim, Tirmīdhī, Aḥmed, Nasa'ī.

[116] Muslim, Dārimī.

[117] Qur'ān 9:111.

وَعْدَ اللهِ حَقًّا ط وَمَنْ اَصْدَقُ مِنَ اللهِ قِيْلًا ○

"The promise of Allāh is true. And who is more true to words than Allāh?" [118]

"With the unseen..." Imām Qurṭubī ﷺ says this could have one of two meanings:

[1] Those who had worshipped Allāh ﷻ and protected his covenant without even seeing Him.

[2] They believed in *Jannah* even though they never saw it, i.e. Allāh ﷻ will reward them for their secret faith.

Verse 62

لَا يَسْمَعُوْنَ فِيْهَا لَغْوًا اِلَّا سَلٰمًا ط
وَلَهُمْ رِزْقُهُمْ فِيْهَا بُكْرَةً وَّعَشِيًّا ﴿٦٢﴾

They will not hear in there anything absurd, but a word of peace.
And they will have their provision there morning and evening.

"They will not hear in there anything absurd, but a word of peace..." لَغو is useless talk which consists of indecent words and in which there is no benefit. [119]

One *Ḥadīth* says, "When the *Imām* is giving *Khuṭbah* on Friday and you say to your friend 'Keep quiet', you have committed *Laghw*" (i.e. If you said something which you should not have said, it would have been better for you to keep quiet and listen attentively).

Ibn 'Abbās ﷺ says:

---

[118] Qur'ān 4:122.

[119] Qurṭubī.

اللَّغْوُ كُلُّ مَا لَمْ يَكُنْ فِيهِ ذِكْرُ اللهِ تَعَالَى .

"Laghw is anything that does not contain the remembrance of Allāh ﷻ."

One *Ḥadīth* says,

لَا تُكْثِرُوا الْكَلَامَ بِغَيْرِ ذِكْرِ اللهِ فَإِنَّ كَثْرَةَ الْكَلَامِ بِغَيْرِ ذِكْرِ اللهِ قَسْوَةٌ لِلْقَلْبِ ، وَإِنَّ أَبْعَدَ النَّاسِ مِنَ اللهِ الْقَلْبُ الْقَاسِي .

"Do not talk excessively with anything besides the remembrance of Allāh, because Abūndance of talk besides the remembrance of Allāh (dhikr) is a cause for the hardening of the heart. And the furthest away from Allāh among all people is the one who is hard hearted." [120]

Another *Ḥadīth* says:

كُلُّ كَلَامِ ابْنِ آدَمَ عَلَيْهِ لَا لَهُ ،
إِلَّا أَمْرٌ بِمَعْرُوفٍ ، أَوْ نَهْيٌ عَنْ مُنْكَرٍ ، أَوْ ذِكْرُ اللهِ .

"Every word of the son of Adam is against him not in his favour except a word which commands good or forbids evil or dhikrullāh." [121]

In this *Dunyā*, we sometimes engage in excessive useless talk. BT had the slogan '*It's good to talk*'. Sometimes we have to put up with useless conversation. In *Jannah*, there will be no useless talk at all.

"Except for peace..." Muqātil رحمه الله explains that they will greet each other with "peace". And Allāh ﷻ will also greet them with *Salām*. In Sūrah Yasīn we read:

سَلٰمٌ قف قَوْلًا مِّنْ رَّبٍّ رَّحِيْمٍ ۝

[120] Mishkāt.

[121] Mishkāt.

"Salām is the word (they will receive) from the merciful Lord." [122]

In Sūrah al-Ra'ad, Allāh says:

وَالْمَلٰئِكَةُ يَدْخُلُوْنَ عَلَيْهِمْ مِّنْ كُلِّ بَابٍ ۝
سَلٰمٌ عَلَيْكُمْ بِمَا صَبَرْتُمْ فَنِعْمَ عُقْبَى الدَّارِ ۝

"And Angels will be entering upon them from every gate. (Saying) 'Peace be upon you for you have surely been patient, now how fitting is (the reward of) the ultimate abode." [123]

In Sūrah Zumar, Allāh ﷻ says,

وَقَالَ لَهُمْ خَزَنَتُهَا سَلٰمٌ عَلَيْكُمْ طِبْتُمْ فَادْخُلُوْهَا خٰلِدِيْنَ ۝

"And the keepers of Jannah will say to them 'Peace be upon you! You have been good, so enter it to live herein forever." [124]

In Sūrah an-Nabā', Allāh ﷻ says:

لَا يَسْمَعُوْنَ فِيْهَا لَغْوًا وَّلَا كِذّٰبًا ۝

"There, they shall hear neither futile talk nor lies." [125]

In Sūrah Al-Wāq'iah, we read:

لَا يَسْمَعُوْنَ فِيْهَا لَغْوًا وَّلَا تَأْثِيْمًا ۝ اِلَّا قِيْلًا سَلٰمًا سَلٰمًا ۝

"They in there will not hear any absurd talk nor anything leading to sin, except the words 'salām, salām'." [126]

---

[122] Qur'ān 36:58.

[123] Qur'ān 13:23-24.

[124] Qur'ān 39:73.

[125] Qur'ān 78:35.

[126] Qur'ān 56:25-26.

"And they will have their provisions their morning and evening..." 'Allāmah 'Uthmānī ﷫ writes, "Here morning and evening means the morning and evening of paradise. There shall be no sunrise or sunset in paradise like that of this world. However, there shall be the showering of special lights by which morning and evening will be calculated. The provisions of *Jannah* will be served morning and evening in the usual manner. There shall be no pain or hunger for a single minute."

A *Ḥadīth* in *Musnad Aḥmad* says, "The martyrs will be on the brilliant shining rivers by the gates of *Jannah*, in green domes, their food will come to them from *Jannah* morning and evening."

[1] Walīd ibn Muslim ﷫ says, "I asked Zuhair ibn Muḥammad regarding this verse and he said, 'In *Jannah*, there is no night, they will always be in *Nūr*. Their times will be estimated by night and day (of the *Dunyā*), they will recognise the night by the lowering of curtains and the closing of doors and recognise the day by the raising of curtains and the opening of doors." [127]

Yaḥyā ibn Kathīr ﷫ and Qatādah ﷫ say that the most wealthy and luxurious person amongst the Arabs was thought to be that person who would receive fresh food morning and evening. Therefore Allāh ﷻ is trying to say they will be enjoying the luxuries of *Jannah* at all times.

[2] Some *Mufassirīn* say that normally, lunch and supper are different. Therefore they will get different varieties of food in order to increase their luxury and enjoyment. Ḥakīm Tirmidhī ﷫ has narrated this *Ḥadīth* in *Nawādir al-Usūl* that someone said, "Yā *Rasūlullāh*! Is there night in *Jannah*?" He asked: "What makes you say this?" The *Ṣaḥābī* ﷜ put forward the above verse and said, "Between evening and morning there is night." *Rasūlullāh* ﷺ replied, "There is no night, but radiance and light. Allāh will turn morning over evening and evening over morning. New presents will be

---

[127] Ibn Kathīr.

brought to them from Allāh according to the times of *Ṣalāh* they had been observing in this *Dunyā* and the angels will be greeting them." [128]

[3] Some *Mufassirīn* say that this is a phrase used for expressing the continuity of their provisions. In Sūrah Wāq'iah, Allāh ﷻ says:

لَّا مَقْطُوْعَةٍ وَّلَا مَمْنُوْعَةٍ ۝

"*Neither interrupted (in any season) nor prohibited.*" [129]

In Sūrah Ḥā-Mīm Sajdah, Allāh ﷻ says,

اِنَّ الَّذِيْنَ اٰمَنُوْا وَعَمِلُوا الصّٰلِحٰتِ لَهُمْ اَجْرٌ غَيْرُ مَمْنُوْنٍ ۝

"*Surely those who believed and worked righteous deeds, for them is a reward which will never be ceased.*" [130]

A *Ḥadīth* of Bukhārī and Muslim narrated by Ibn Kathīr رحمه الله says, "The first group who enter *Jannah*, their faces will be (radiant) like the full moon. Therein they will not spit, nor will they blow their noses, nor will they relieve themselves. Their utensils as well as their combs will be of pure gold and silver. Their thurible (censer) will be o'ūd (aloeswood). Their perspiration will be (like) musk. Each one will have two wives, the marrow of their shins will be visible in spite of flesh, due to their beauty. There will be no arguments amongst them nor any malice held. Their hearts will be like the heart of one single person. They will glorify Allāh morning and evening."

Glorifying Allāh ﷻ will be a continuous act as another *Ḥadīth* highlights, "They will be inspired to glorify just as you are inspired to breathe." i.e. a person breathes continuously and at the same time, he goes about doing his work. Similarly, the *Tasbīh* of *Ahl al-Jannah* will flow continuously. The luxuries of *Jannah* will never distract them from glorifying Allāh ﷻ. In the

[128] Qurṭubī.

[129] Qur'ān 56:33.

[130] Qur'ān 41:8.

same way, the provisions of *Jannah* will be served continuously without ceasing.

VERSE 63

$$ تِلْكَ الْجَنَّةُ الَّتِيْ نُوْرِثُ مِنْ عِبَادِنَا مَنْ كَانَ تَقِيًّا ﴿٦٣﴾ $$

That is the Jannah We will give as inheritance to those of Our servants who have been God-fearing.

"*That is the Jannah...*" Ibn Kathīr ﷫ says, تَقِيّ here means one who is obedient to Allāh ﷻ in happiness and in distress, who suppresses his anger and pardons people – such people will inherit *Jannah* as mentioned in the opening verses of Sūrah Al-Mu'minūn.

"*We give its inheritance to one who is god fearing...*" Shah Walīullāh ﷫ writes, "There is no doubt that when Sūrah Maryam was revealed in Makkah Mukarramah, many amongst the Jews and Christians were such who had deviated from the path of Mūsā ﷵ and 'Īsā ﷵ. They had abandoned *Ṣalāh* and followed their whimsical desires. However, there were those who were classed as God-fearing: They possessed correct belief and they performed righteous deeds. They deserved to be called the God-fearing. They are the *Ṣaḥābah*, the *Muhājirīn* who were forced out of their homes by the oppressors amongst the *Quraysh*. They will be the first inheritors of *Jannah*. This proves the status of the *Ṣaḥābah*." [131]

Verses 64-65

$$ وَمَا نَتَنَزَّلُ اِلَّا بِاَمْرِ رَبِّكَ ۚ لَهُ مَا بَيْنَ اَيْدِيْنَا وَمَا خَلْفَنَا وَمَا بَيْنَ ذٰلِكَ ۚ وَمَا كَانَ رَبُّكَ نَسِيًّا ﴿٦٤﴾ رَبُّ السَّمٰوٰتِ وَالْاَرْضِ وَمَا بَيْنَهُمَا فَاعْبُدْهُ وَاصْطَبِرْ لِعِبَادَتِهٖ $$

---

[131] Izālat al-Khifā.

ط هَلْ تَعْلَمُ لَهُ سَمِيًّا ﴿٦٥﴾

And we (the angels) do not descend except by the command of your Lord. His is whatever is in front of us and whatever is behind us and whatever is in between. And your Lord is never forgetful. Lord of the heavens and the earth and what is in between; so, worship Him and endure patiently in His worship. Do you know of anyone similar to Him?

"*And we do not descend...*" In the previous verses, prophets and their devotion was narrated. Now Allāh ﷻ is mentioning the devotion of the angels and their being dutiful to the commands of Allāh ﷻ.

Ibn 'Ạbbās ؓ says that *Rasūlullāh* ﷺ said to Jibrā'īl ؑ:

مَا يَمْنَعُكَ أَنْ تَزُورَنَا أَكْثَرَ مِمَّا تَزُورُنَا.

"*What prevents you from visiting us more frequently?*"

Upon this Allāh ﷻ revealed, "*We do not descend except by the command of your Lord.*" [132]

Ạṭīyyah al-Awfī ؒ narrated from 'Ibn 'Ạbbās ؓ that Jibrā'īl ؑ stayed away from *Rasūlullāh* ﷺ (for a few days). He ﷺ was aggrieved and was in a sorry state. Jibrā'īl ؑ came with the above verses.

Mujāhid, Qatādah, Ịkrimah, Ḍhaḥḥāk ؒ and others narrate that when the *Mushrikīn* of Makkah enquired about the *Aṣ'ḥāb al-Kahf* (the Sleepers of the Cave) and Dhul-Qarnayn, the Prophet ﷺ promised to give a reply by the next day. He thought that he would be able to ask Jibrā'īl ؑ and give the answer. However, he forgot to say '*Inshā'-Allāh*'. This resulted in Jibrā'īl ؑ being held back for fifteen days. The polytheists of Makkah began to make a mockery of him. When Jibrā'īl ؑ finally arrived, the Prophet ﷺ asked him the reason for the delay, upon which Jibrā'īl ؑ came with the verse in discussion. [133]

---

[132] Bukḥārī, Muslim.

[133] Qurṭubī.

Ḥaḍhrat Maulānā Idrīs Kāndhalwī ۔ writes, "In these verses Allāh ۔ first instructs us to worship Him and then He says be patient in worship. The reason is that there are two ranks here. One is of *Abdiyyah* which means to become a slave. The second is *'Ubūdiyyah* i.e. to endure patience and be steadfast in that condition. This means that performing *Ṣalāh* once in a while is not enough. What is required is consistency, perpetuated worship; to be engaged constantly in such a manner that one does not move away from the worship for a single moment."

Another point to be noted here is that Allāh ۔ is the *Rabb* of the heavens and the earth. This is to show the reason why He deserves to be worshipped, i.e. due to His looking after and taking care of the whole universe, He deserves our worship.

'Allāmah 'Uthmānī ۔ writes, "These words (i.e. we do not descend but...) are the words of Allāh ۔ from the side of Jibrā'īl ۔. They are the same as what we have been taught in the first Sūrah: اياك نعبد - 'Only you do we worship and from only you do we seek help.'"

The substance of the answer is that the angels are absolutely obedient servants and cannot move even a little without the order of Allāh ۔. Their ascension and descent is subject to divine order. Whenever He deems fit, according to His perfect wisdom, He orders them to come down because He alone has the knowledge of the time (past, present, and future) and He alone has the knowledge of space (heavens and earth and what is in between them). He is the absolute owner of everything and He alone knows the best time to send the angel to the messenger. The nearest of the angels and the most revered of the prophets do not have the power to go anywhere they like or call out to anyone they want to. The action of God Himself is in accordance to circumstances and occasions. Forgetfulness, heedlessness, or mistakes do not reach His glorious self. He may delay something for reasons best known to Him.

[1] Ḥaḍhrat Muftī 'Āshiq Ilāhī ۔ writes in *Bayān al-Qur'ān*, "Some commentators say that *'whatever is before us'* refers to the future, *'whatever is*

behind us' refers to the past, and '*whatever is between the two*' refers to the present."

[2] Abū Laylā ﷺ says that '*before us*' refers to the entire universe before the blowing of the trumpet, '*behind us*' refers to the hereafter and '*between the two*' refers to the time between the first blowing of the trumpet and the second blowing. This intermediate period will last fourty [40] years.

[3] Some commentators say '*before us*' refers to the earth (because when an angel is descending, the earth is before him) and '*behind us*' refers to the skies (which he has left behind). The next verse indicates towards this, "*The Rabb of the heavens and the earth and whatever is in between.*"

The conclusion is that Allāh ﷻ is in control of all places and all times. None may move from one place to another without Allāh's ﷻ will.

"*And your Rabb never forgets...*" Mujāhid ﷺ says, "*This means that He has not forgotten you.*"

"*So worship Him and be patient in His worship...*" Tafsīr Mazharī states, "*This means, 'Do not worry about the scolding of the disbelievers. Keep yourself busy in Allāh's ﷻ worship.*" Allāh ﷻ says in Sūrah al-Ḥijr:

وَلَقَدْ نَعْلَمُ اَنَّكَ يَضِيْقُ صَدْرُكَ بِمَا يَقُوْلُوْنَ ۝ فَسَبِّحْ بِحَمْدِ
رَبِّكَ وَكُنْ مِّنَ السّٰجِدِيْنَ ۝ وَاعْبُدْ رَبَّكَ حَتّٰى يَاْتِيَكَ الْيَقِيْنُ ۝

"*We know for sure that your heart is troubled by what they say. So glorify your Lord along with His praise and be of those who prostrate. And worship your Lord until certainty (death) comes to you.*" [134]

[134] Qur'ān 15:97-99.

In Sūrah al-Nahl, Allāh ﷻ says,

وَاصْبِرْ وَمَا صَبْرُكَ إِلَّا بِاللهِ وَلَا تَحْزَنْ عَلَيْهِمْ وَلَا تَكُ فِىْ ضَيْقٍ مِّمَّا
يَمْكُرُوْنَ ۝ إِنَّ اللهَ مَعَ الَّذِيْنَ اتَّقَوْا وَالَّذِيْنَ هُمْ مُّحْسِنُوْنَ ۝

"And be patient and your patience is not possible except by the help of Allāh and do not grieve upon them, and do not be troubled by their plotting. Verily Allāh is with those who are pious and those who do virtue." [135]

There is a great lesson in these verses for every one of us. Whenever we feel low and face any form of mockery or persecution, we should immediately turn our attention towards the Almighty Allāh ﷻ. Our worship should increase. We should show our devotion to Allāh ﷻ and He alone is the one who will remove our difficulties. We have to write with great regret that people today come up with various suggestions but fail to mention the root cause of our problems i.e. our detachment from Allāh ﷻ. We have gone so far away that we don't think about Allāh ﷻ when we face any difficulty. We say Muslims should do this, they should do that. May Allāh ﷻ have mercy on us and give us the true understanding. *Āmīn.*

"Do you know of anyone similar to him . . ." This could hold two meanings:

[1] Anyone who has beautiful names like Him. The Idolaters would give many different names to the Idols but they never called anyone Allāh or even Raḥmān. Allāh ﷻ has 99 beautiful names. They are exclusively attached to Allāh ﷻ. This is narrated from Ibn 'Abbās رضي الله عنهما.

[2] 'Alī ibn Abī Ṭālib رضي الله عنه says, "This means anyone who could be compared to Him. Anyone who possesses the same attributes as Allāh ﷻ." [136]

---

[135] Qur'ān 16:127-128.

[136] Ibn Kathīr.

The words '*Do you know of anyone similar to him*' are to remove any obstacles from the path of worship, i.e. if there was anyone like Him, one could have said why should I not worship the other God. But since there is no one that can be compared with Him, there is no reason why we should even think about anyone else.

VERSES 66-67

وَيَقُولُ الْإِنْسَانُ ءَإِذَا مَا مِتُّ لَسَوْفَ أُخْرَجُ حَيًّا ﴿٦٦﴾ أَوَلَا يَذْكُرُ
الْإِنْسَانُ أَنَّا خَلَقْنَٰهُ مِنْ قَبْلُ وَلَمْ يَكُ شَيْئًا ﴿٦٧﴾

And man says: Is it the case that when I am dead I shall be raised up alive. Does man not remember that We created him before, while he was nothing.

"*And man says...*" Connection to the previous verses: In the previous verses Allāh ﷻ mentioned the final ending of the righteous and the evil. In these verses, Allāh ﷻ is mentioning the fact that this outcome will be brought to them in the hereafter. People have objections in life after death, therefore, Allāh ﷻ is answering their questions.

Allāh ﷻ is saying that this rejection of the hereafter is due to heedlessness, negligence, and the following of whimsical desires. When a person is engrossed in pleasures and luxuries, his mind stops working and he fails to realise that he was nothing and it is Allāh ﷻ who created him from a drop of semen. When it is possible for Allāh ﷻ to create him the first time, why is it not possible for Allāh to recreate him after death?

There are many narrations in this regard within the Qur'ān and *Ḥadīth*. Allāh ﷻ says in Sūrah Yā-Sīn:

أَوَلَمْ يَرَ الْإِنْسَانُ أَنَّا خَلَقْنَٰهُ مِنْ نُّطْفَةٍ فَإِذَا هُوَ خَصِيمٌ مُّبِينٌ ○
وَضَرَبَ لَنَا مَثَلًا وَّنَسِيَ خَلْقَهُ ط قَالَ مَنْ يُّحْيِ الْعِظَامَ وَهِيَ رَمِيمٌ ○

قُلْ يُحْيِيهَا الَّذِىٓ أَنشَأَهَآ أَوَّلَ مَرَّةٍ ۖ وَهُوَ بِكُلِّ خَلْقٍ عَلِيمٌ ۝

"Has man not seen that we created him from a drop of fluid, yet he is suddenly an open disputer? And he puts forth to us a parable and forgets his own creation. He says: 'Who will breathe life into these bones after they have decomposed?' Say: The one who gave life to them the first time will bring them back to life, And He has full knowledge of every creation." [137]

Allāh ﷻ says,

وَهُوَ الَّذِى يَبْدَؤُا الْخَلْقَ ثُمَّ يُعِيدُهُۥ وَهُوَ أَهْوَنُ عَلَيْهِ ۚ
وَلَهُ الْمَثَلُ الْأَعْلَىٰ فِى السَّمٰوٰتِ وَالْأَرْضِ ۚ وَهُوَ الْعَزِيزُ الْحَكِيمُ ۝

"And it is He who originates the creation then He will reproduce it, and this is very easy for Him. And His is the loftiest state in the heavens and the earth, And He is Mighty, the Wise." [138]

Creating something from nothing is much harder in our perception than gathering some parts which are separated. It is a difficult task for an engineer to construct a fifty storey building. However, if after completion, he was told to make a similar building next to it, this would be much easier for him. Repairing would also be much easier. Big Ben was made 150 years ago. It is now being repaired. This seems much easier than the original construction. So this is a simple fact we have before our very eyes, however, people do not ponder over this.

In one *Ḥadīth al-Qudsī* in *Ṣaḥīḥ al-Bukhārī*, Allāh ﷻ says, "The son of Ādam denies me when he has no right to deny me. The son of Ādam hurts me when he has no right to hurt me. As for his denial, it is his statement that, 'God will never recreate me as He did for the first time.' Whereas the first creation is not easier for me than the last one. As for his hurting me, it is his saying that

[137] Qur'ān 36:77-79.

[138] Qur'ān 30:27.

I have a son, whereas I am the One Alone, the Self-Sufficient whom all creatures need, who has not given birth nor was He born and to whom there is none comparable."

Since people are in denial, Allāh ﷻ has repeatedly mentioned this *Aqīdah* in the Noble Qur'ān. From among the 114 chapters of the Qur'ān, belief in the *Ākhirah* is mentioned to some degree in 67 chapters. Some *sūrahs* are exclusively for narrating the state of affairs of the Day of *Qiyāmah*. In the following verse in connection, Allāh ﷻ takes an oath and says, "*By your Rabb, we will definitely gather them.*"

We have to say with great sadness that many Muslims may not deny life after death; however, their actions are akin to those who have no belief.

The above mentioned clarification is for those who believe in God. As for those who deny the existence of God, it would seem an impossible task to explain to them. All we can do is pray for their guidance.

VERSES 68-69

فَوَرَبِّكَ لَنَحْشُرَنَّهُمْ وَالشَّيٰطِيْنَ ثُمَّ لَنُحْضِرَنَّهُمْ
حَوْلَ جَهَنَّمَ جِثِيًّا ﴿٦٨﴾ ثُمَّ لَنَنْزِعَنَّ مِنْ كُلِّ شِيْعَةٍ
اَيُّهُمْ اَشَدُّ عَلَى الرَّحْمٰنِ عِتِيًّا ﴿٦٩﴾

By your Rabb, We shall definitely gather them, as well as the devils, then We will surely bring them around Jahannam, kneeling. Then We will definitely draw aside, from each sect those who were most rebellious against Al-Raḥmān (the Compassionate).

"*By your Rabb...*" Allāh ﷻ has taken such an oath on many occasions. In Sūrah at-Taghābun, Allāh ﷻ says:

زَعَمَ الَّذِيْنَ كَفَرُوْآ اَنْ لَّنْ يُّبْعَثُوْا ؕ قُلْ بَلٰى وَرَبِّىْ لَتُبْعَثُنَّ

ثُمَّ لَتُنَبَّؤُنَّ بِمَا عَمِلْتُمْ ط وَذٰلِكَ عَلَى اللّٰهِ يَسِيْرٌ ۝

"The disbelievers claim that they will never be raised. Say: "Certainly, by my Lord, you shall be raised, then you shall be informed of what you had done. And this is easy for Allāh." [139]

In Sūrah Yūnus, Allāh ﷻ says:

وَيَسْتَنْۢبِئُوْنَكَ اَحَقٌّ هُوَ ط قُلْ اِيْ وَرَبِّيْٓ اِنَّهٗ لَحَقٌّ ط وَمَا اَنْتُمْ بِمُعْجِزِيْنَ ۝

"And they ask you, 'Is this true?" Say, 'Yes! By my Lord! It is surely the truth, and you will not escape.'" [140]

In Sūrah adh-Dhāriyāh, Allāh ﷻ says:

فَوَرَبِّ السَّمَآءِ وَالْاَرْضِ اِنَّهٗ لَحَقٌّ مِّثْلَ مَآ اَنَّكُمْ تَنْطِقُوْنَ ۝

"By the Lord of the sky and the earth, it is definitely true, just as you are speaking (We do not need to be convinced of our speech)." [141]

"We shall definitely gather them, as well as the devils..." This means the deniers will be brought along with the devils who used to mislead them. Every human has an angel who calls him towards good and a devil who encourages him to do evil. On the Day of Judgement, the devil will be chained with the disbeliever and they will come together. [142]

"Then we will surely bring them around Jahannam, kneeling..." Allāh ﷻ says in Sūrah al-Jāthiyah,

وَتَرٰى كُلَّ اُمَّةٍ جَاثِيَةً قف كُلُّ اُمَّةٍ تُدْعٰٓى اِلٰى كِتٰبِهَا ط

اَلْيَوْمَ تُجْزَوْنَ مَا كُنْتُمْ تَعْمَلُوْنَ ۝ هٰذَا كِتٰبُنَا يَنْطِقُ عَلَيْكُمْ

[139] Qur'ān 64:7.

[140] Qur'ān 10:53.

[141] Qur'ān 51:23.

[142] Ma'ārif al-Qur'ān Kāndhalwī.

بِالْحَقِّ ط اِنَّا كُنَّا نَسْتَنْسِخُ مَا كُنْتُمْ تَعْمَلُوْنَ ۝

"You shall see every nation on its knees. Every nation shall be summoned to its book, and a voice will say: 'You shall on this day be rewarded for your deeds. This book of ours speaks with truth against you. We have recorded all your actions." [143]

'Allāmah 'Uthmānī writes, "Due to their horrific state, they will fall helplessly on their knees, they will not be able to sit with ease, or even stand on their feet."

Anwār al-Bayān states, "This will serve to intensify their humiliation before actually entering *Jahannam*. All the rejecters, irrespective of their positions in the world will be there together. However, sifting will then take place." That is why Allāh says: "*Then We will separate from every group those who were most rebellious against Raḥmān.*"

Every gang has one or many leaders. The leaders will be the first to be thrown into the fire. *Jahannam* is extremely deep, and the worst punishment is in the lowest part. Therefore, the leaders will be thrown in first and the followers will follow. Allāh says in Sūrah an-Nahl:

اَلَّذِيْنَ كَفَرُوْا وَصَدُّوْا عَنْ سَبِيْلِ اللّٰهِ زِدْنٰهُمْ
عَذَابًا فَوْقَ الْعَذَابِ بِمَا كَانُوْا يُفْسِدُوْنَ ۝

"Verily those who disbelieved and hindered others from the path of Allāh, We shall add punishment to their punishment because of the corruption they had caused." [144]

The word شِيْعَة literally means group. In a much broader sense, it means, 'a group who hold a special belief or who follow a single leader.' [145]

Ibn Abī Ḥātim and Bayhaqī have narrated the following from Ibn Mas'ūd, "When humans will all be resurrected from the first to the last,

[143] Qur'ān 45:28-29.

[144] Qur'ān 16:88.

[145] Ma'arij Mufti Shafī Ṣāḥib.

their counting will be completed, then they will be sifted through, beginning with major criminals and coming down to the smaller ones." [146]

VERSE 70

ثُمَّ لَنَحْنُ اَعْلَمُ بِالَّذِيْنَ هُمْ اَوْلٰى بِهَا صِلِيًّا ﴿٧٠﴾

Then, verily, We know best those who are most worthy of being burnt in there.

"Then, verily We know best those who are most worthy of being burnt in there..." 'Ạllāmah 'Ụthmānī ﵀ writes, "Amongst the various sects of disbelievers, the most wicked and arrogant ringleaders shall be plucked out of other criminals. And among those ringleaders, one who will be more wicked and disdainful in the knowledge of Allāh shall be thrown first into the hellfire to burn."

Ibn Kathīr ﵀ writes, "Allāh ﷻ knows best which of His creatures deserve to be burnt in the fire of Hell and remain there forever and who deserves to have his punishment doubled."

VERSE 71

وَاِنْ مِّنْكُمْ اِلَّا وَارِدُهَا ۚ كَانَ عَلٰى رَبِّكَ حَتْمًا مَّقْضِيًّا ﴿٧١﴾

There is not one of you who shall not pass through it: Such is the absolute decree of your Lord.

"There is not one of you..." 'Ạllāmah 'Ụthmānī ﵀ writes, "For every human being, bad or good, criminal or acquitted, believer or disbeliever, Allāh ﷻ has said an oath and made a solemn decree that they shall surely pass over *Jahannam*, because the way to *Jannah* lies over *Jahannam*. (*Jahannam* will be brought closer to the plain of resurrection and the *Maydān* of *Ḥashr* will be

---

[146] Mazharī.

surrounded by *Jahannam*). In order to cross over to *Jannah*, each soul will have to cross the bridge which is commonly known as *Pul-Ṣirāṭ* (bridge-way)."

Those who had feared Allāh ﷻ will cross swiftly according to the degree of their ranks. (Some as quickly as the blink of an eye, others like the flash of lightning, others like a heavy wind, others like fast running horses, some like fast camels). The sinners will fall into *Jahannam*. (The *Pul-Ṣirāṭ* will be surrounded by massive hooks. They will catch and injure the sinful ones who will finally tumble over into *Jahannam*. These hooks will in reality be the sins which they had committed. They shall come to haunt them and hinder their crossing). Then after some time by the blessing of their good deeds, those who had the correct belief will be taken out of *Jahannam* according to their actions. Also some will be taken out by the intercession of the Prophets, the Angels, and pious servants. Then finally there will be some, who due to their excessive sinning, will not be recognised by any of the above. They will be taken out by none but the *Arḥam ar-Rāḥimīn* (The Most Merciful Among Those Who Show Mercy). Only the disbelievers, the deniers and rejecters shall remain there, and the doors of *Jahannam* will be closed upon them.

Some *Aḥādīth* (narrations) indicate that the believers will also have to go to visit *Jahannam*. However, the fire will become cool and peaceful for them just as it had done so for *Sayyidunā* Ibrāhīm al-Khalīl ﷺ when he was thrown into the fire by the tyrant Namrūd (Nimrod). This visit will be so that they can realise the severity of Allāh's ﷻ punishment and therefore thank Allāh ﷻ and be grateful for saving them from the punishment. In his *Tafsīr*, Imām Fakhruddīn Rāzī رحمه الله has mentioned much wisdom behind this visit.

Imām Muslim رحمه الله narrates from *Ummul Mu'minīn* Ḥafṣah رضي الله عنها that *Rasūlullāh* ﷺ said, "From amongst those who participated in *Badr* and *Ḥudaibīyyah*, none will enter the fire..." Ḥafṣah رضي الله عنها says, "I said *Yā Rasūlullāh* ﷺ, then what about Allāh's saying, 'There is none amongst you who will not enter it'?" He replied, "Read what is after." "Then we will rescue those who had *Taqwā*," i.e. they will not go there to be punished.

Rasūlullāh ﷺ meant that none among *Ahl al-Badr* and the *Ahl al-Ḥudaibiyyah* will be punished. Maulānā 'Abdul Mājid Daryabādī ﵀ writes in *Tafsīr Mājidī*, "Compare a teaching of Jesus unrecorded in the canonised gospels:
"Everyone be he who must go into Hell. It is true, however that the Holy Ones and Prophets of God shall go there to behold, not suffering any punishment."
147

Many amongst the Salaf used to ponder over this entry into *Jahannam* and then cry.

'Abdullāh ibn Rawāḥah ﵁ was once ill. His head was in the lap of his wife. He started crying and she also began to cry. 'Abdullāh ibn Rawāḥah ﵁ enquired as to the reason for her tears. She replied, "I saw you crying, which brought tears to my eyes." He replied thus, "I pondered over these words, "From amongst those who participated in *Badr* and *Ḥudaibiyyah*, none will enter the fire..." I don't know whether I will be amongst those who are taken out safely or not."

Abū Maysarah ﵁ would come to his bed and then suddenly start crying. He would say, "I wish my mother would never have given birth to me." Someone enquired about the reason for his anxiety and he replied, "We have been informed that you will definitely visit *Jahannam*, however, there is no such wording to say you will get out of there."

Ḥasan Baṣrī ﵀ says that one *Ṣaḥābī* ﵁ saw his brother laughing loudly. He asked, "Have you been told that you will definitely enter *Jahannam*?" He replied in the affirmative. The *Ṣaḥābī* ﵁ questioned, "Have you any confirmation that you will get out of it?" He replied, "No." The *Ṣaḥābī* ﵁ said, "Then why this laughter?" Ḥasan Baṣrī ﵀ states that after this incident, no one ever saw him laughing.

Maulānā Amīr 'Alī writes in *Tafsīr Mawāhib Ar-Raḥmān*, "This is due to severe fear of Allāh ﷻ and due to their strong *yaqīn* (belief) in the words of Allāh ﷻ."

---

147 G.B. Pg. 159.

Shaddād ibn ʿAws would toss and turn on his bed. He would say that the fear of *Jahannam* has driven my sleep away. Then he would get up and pray all night.

Muḥammad ibn al-Munkadir ﵁ would cry and then wet his face and beard with the tears that flowed from his eyes. He would say, "I have heard that the Fire of *Jahannam* will not burn those areas where tears of the eyes have passed."

VERSE 72

ثُمَّ نُنَجِّى الَّذِينَ اتَّقَوا وَّنَذَرُ الظَّالِمِينَ فِيهَا جِثِيًّا ﴿٧٢﴾

Then We will rescue those who had Taqwā, but We shall leave the wrongdoers there on their knees.

"*Then We will rescue those who had Taqwā...*" This shows the excellence of *Taqwā*, which means fear of Allāh ﷻ, constant awareness of the presence of Allāh ﷻ, and complete obedience to every command of Allāh ﷻ. Some of the *Mashāikh* say that *Taqwā* is a collection of four attributes:

الخوف من الجليل و العمل بالتنزيل

و القناعة بالقليل و الإستعداد ليوم الرحيل .

"Fear of the Mighty Lord, practice upon what he has revealed, be content with little provisions of the Dunyā and finally, preparation for the Day of Journey."

Junaid Baghdādī ﵁ says, "Whoever is rescued, it will be due to the sincerity of the Heart." Ḥarīrī ﵁ says, "Salvation will be through *Ṣidq* and *Taqwā* (i.e. Sincerity and the fear of Allāh ﷻ)."

Ibn ʿAṭā ﵁ says, "Those who were true to their words and fulfilled the Covenant will be saved."

Some say, "Only the grace of the Almighty will come to the rescue, all other things are just means provided by the Almighty."

Imām Jạ'far al-Ṣādiq ﷺ says, "If there was no connection with the ego, then no one would have gone to *Jahannam*. The close attachment to the ego (*Nafs*) pushed them towards *Jahannam*. Therefore, whomsoever abstains from the desires of the ego and shows patience in obedience will swiftly cross over *Jahannam*." [148]

VERSE 73

وَاِذَا تُتْلٰى عَلَيْهِمْ اٰيٰتُنَا بَيِّنٰتٍ قَالَ الَّذِيْنَ كَفَرُوْا لِلَّذِيْنَ

اٰمَنُوْا لا اَیُّ الْفَرِيْقَيْنِ خَيْرٌ مَّقَامًا وَّاَحْسَنُ نَدِيًّا ﴿٧٣﴾

And when Our clear verses are recited to them, the Disbelievers say to the Believers, "Which of the two groups is superior in its place and better in its assembly?"

"And when our clear verses..." This means that when the Qur'ān is recited to the disbelievers, they laugh at it, and make a mockery of it. Allāh ﷻ says in Sūrah Ḥā-Mīm Sajdah, "And the disbelievers said, "Do not listen to this Qur'ān, but talk at random in the midst of it, so that you may gain the upper hand." [149]

They take pride in their beautiful houses and their well-attended gatherings. They take it as an argument in favour of their disbelief and sinful acts. They claim that if we were wrong, then God would not have blessed us with this prosperity. They would say, "Are our houses, furniture, and other possessions not better than yours? Is our society not superior to your society? You say we are wrong, but we wrong people are more powerful than you righteous men. How can we believe that those who are restricted in an area around Mount *Ṣafā* today, shall jump into Paradise tomorrow and leave us burning in Hell?"

This is the same argument which Pharaoh put forward. Allāh ﷻ says in Sūrah ash-Shūrā, "And Pharaoh proclaimed amongst his people saying, "O my People, does not the dominion of Egypt belong to me? And (look at) these

---

[148] Mawāhib Ar-Raḥmān, Vol 16, Pg. 220.

[149] Qur'ān 41:26.

streams flowing beneath me (my palaces). Do you then not see? Am I not better than this one (i.e. Mūsā ﷺ) who is a contemptible wretch, and can scarcely express himself clearly? Then why are gold bracelets not bestowed upon him, or why are the Angels not coming to him in succession? Thus did he make fools of his people, and they obeyed him. Truly; they were a rebellious nation." [150]

VERSE 74

وَكَمْ اَهْلَكْنَا قَبْلَهُمْ مِّنْ قَرْنٍ هُمْ اَحْسَنُ اَثَاثًا وَّرِءْيًا ﴿٧٤﴾

But how many generations (i.e. countless) We have destroyed before them, who were even better in equipment and in outward appearance.

"But how many Generations..." 'Ạllāmah 'Ụthmānī ﷺ writes, "This is an answer to the proud assertions of the disbelievers. There have been many generations who possessed more wealth and provisions and who displayed more pomp and show than these people. But when they became haughty and adopted the way of vanity against the Prophets, God annihilated them from the face of this Earth. Generally the proud and the wealthy men become the target of destruction when they oppose the truth and prefer tyranny over justice. Wealth and children and worldly prosperity is not the cause of acceptability and of an excellent ending." [151]

Ibn Kathīr ﷺ narrates from 'Ạbdullāh ibn 'Ạbbās ﷺ that he said, "Position ('*Maqām*') means home, "*Nadīy*" means place of gathering, "wealth" refers to material possessions and outward appearance is how they look physically."

[150] Qur'ān 43:51-54.

[151] Pg. 1403.

Verse 75

قُلْ مَنْ كَانَ فِى الضَّلٰلَةِ فَلْيَمْدُدْ لَهُ الرَّحْمٰنُ مَدًّا ۚ حَتّٰىٓ اِذَا رَاَوْا مَا يُوْعَدُوْنَ اِمَّا
الْعَذَابَ وَاِمَّا السَّاعَةَ ؕ فَسَيَعْلَمُوْنَ مَنْ هُوَ شَرٌّ مَّكَانًا وَّاَضْعَفُ جُنْدًا ﴿٧٥﴾

Say, "Whosoever goes astray, then let (Allāh) the most gracious extend (the rope) to them. Until when they see that with which they were warned - either the punishment or (the approach of) The Hour, then they will realise who is worse in position and weaker in forces.

"Say whosoever goes astray..." 'Ạllāmah 'Ụthmānī ﷬ writes, "Whosoever goes into error, then let him go because this world is a place of examinations. Allāh ﷻ has given freedom to all actions to a certain degree. The custom and wisdom of the Almighty make it necessary that when a person wants to go on a certain path, then he should be informed of the good or bad nature of that path and then be allowed to do so, but up to a certain degree. Therefore, when a person opts for an evil path and yet he is provided with the luxuries and long life, then this should be deemed as a prelude to his destruction. In this world, the good and bad are intermingled. They will be totally separated in the Hereafter where the real virtue or vice will be repaid."

Q

What is the wisdom behind this let off?

A

[1] When a person abandons the Hereafter for this *Dunyā*, then he should be given what he desires.

[2] When the wealthy indulge in luxuries, then they will oppress the dutiful servants, then their patience will be put to a test.

[3] This way the excuses of the disbelievers will be finished. They will not be able to say that they did not get enough time to ponder and accept the truth.

Q

Why did Allāh ﷻ use the attribute "*al-Raḥmān*?"

A

To show that their disobedience and rebellious nature should have resulted in their immediate destruction. However, it is the mercy of The Merciful which has given them respite. This attribute '*Ar-Raḥmān*' has been used sixteen times in this Sūrah. [152]

"*Until when they see that with which they were warned...*" 'Allāmah 'Uthmānī رحمه الله writes, "The disbelievers think that the Muslims are weak and contemptible whereas they are dignified and strong. They gloat over their splendid houses and strong armies. This is due to the respite that Allāh ﷻ has given them. As soon as they are gripped either through punishment in this *Dunyā* or the Hereafter, they will realise whose position was more contemptible and who was weaker. At that moment no amount of armies or possessions will come to benefit them." [153]

VERSE 76

وَيَزِيْدُ اللهُ الَّذِيْنَ اهْتَدَوْا هُدًى ط وَالْبٰقِيٰتُ

الصّٰلِحٰتُ خَيْرٌ عِنْدَ رَبِّكَ ثَوَابًا وَّخَيْرٌ مَّرَدًّا ﴿٧٦﴾

And Allāh does increase in guidance those who want to be guided. And the everlasting virtuous deeds are better with your Lord in respect of reward and better in their

---

[152] Mawāhib Ar-Raḥmān.

[153] Pg. 1401.

eventual returns.

"And Allāh does increase in guidance..." This means that upon the recitation of the clear verses of Allāh 🕮, people fall into two categories. One is of those who make fun in their wrongdoing, thus sinning and further deviating. The second group is of those whose guidance (*Hidāyah*) is increased. Their *Īmān* is strengthened. Allāh 🕮 says in another place in Sūrah Tawbah:

> "Whenever there comes down a *surah*, some of them say: "Which of you has had his faith increased by it?" As for those who believe, their faith is increased and they do rejoice. But those in whose heart is a disease, - it will add doubt to their doubt, and they will die in a state of unbelief."

"And the everlasting virtuous deeds are better." وَالْبَاقِيَاتُ الصَّالِحَاتُ has been explained in Sūrah Kahf.

[1] Ibn ʿAbbās 🕮 and Saʿīd ibn Jubayr 🕮, among other scholars, say that they are the five daily *Ṣalāh*.

[2] ʿAṭā ibn Abī Rabāḥ and Saʿīd ibn Jubayr 🕮 narrate from Ibn ʿAbbās in another narration that they are ʿSubḥānAllāh, Alḥamdulillāh, Allāhu Akbar.'

[3] *Amīr al-Muʾminīn* ʿUthmān ibn ʿAffān 🕮 was asked, "What are the everlasting deeds?" He replied, "They are *Lā ilāha illAllāh, SubḥānAllāh, Alḥamdulillāh, Allāhu Akbar* and *Lā ḥawla wa la quwwata illā billāhil ʿAlīyyil ʿAẓīm.*"

Imām Aḥmad 🕮 narrates a *Ḥadīth* in which *Rasūlullāh* 🕮 said, "How excellent are five things! How weighty they are in scale, *'Lā ilāha illAllāh, Allāhu Akbar, Subḥān Allāh, Alḥamdulillāh,* and a righteous son who dies and his father is (patient while) seeking reward from Allāh."

'Alī ibn Abī Ṭalḥah ﷺ reported from Ibn 'Abbās ﷺ who said, "This is the celebration of the remembrance of Allāh ﷻ by saying '*Lā ilāha illAllāh, Allāhu Akbar, Subḥān Allāh, Alḥamdulillāh, TabārakAllāh, Lā ḥawla wa la quwwata illā billāh, Astaghfirullah, ṢallAllāhu 'ạlā Rasūlillaāh* and fasting, prayer, *Ḥajj*, *Ṣadaqah*, freeing slaves, *Jiḥād*, maintaining ties of kinship and all other good deeds. These are the righteous good deeds which last, which will remain in paradise for those who do them for as long as heaven and earth remain."

Al-Awfī ﷺ narrated from Ibn 'Abbās ﷺ, "They are good words." Zaid Ibn Aslam says, "They are all righteous deeds."

"*Are better with your Lord...*" Their reward is far greater and they will bring a better return than the splendour of this *Dunyā*. The lofty ranks and armies over which these people are boasting will not survive, however the virtues and rewards of the simple words of *dhikrullāh* shall remain forever.

VERSES 77-80

أَفَرَءَيْتَ الَّذِى كَفَرَ بِـَٔايَـٰتِنَا وَقَالَ لَأُوتَيَنَّ مَالًا وَوَلَدًا ﴿٧٧﴾ أَطَّلَعَ الْغَيْبَ أَمِ
اتَّخَذَ عِندَ الرَّحْمَـٰنِ عَهْدًا ﴿٧٨﴾ كَلَّا ۚ سَنَكْتُبُ مَا يَقُولُ وَنَمُدُّ لَهُۥ مِنَ الْعَذَابِ
مَدًّا ﴿٧٩﴾ وَنَرِثُهُۥ مَا يَقُولُ وَيَأْتِينَا فَرْدًا ﴿٨٠﴾

"Have you seen the one who rejected Our Āyah (signs, verses) and said: "I shall certainly be given wealth and children (if I live again)? Has he peeked to the unseen or has he taken a promise from the most gracious? Never! We shall record what he says and We shall intensify the punishment for him. And We shall inherit from him all that he speaks of and he shall come to Us alone.

"*Have you seen the one . . .*" In the previous verses, Allāh ﷻ gave the answer to the boasting of the *Mushrikīn* (polytheists) over their wealth and properties. In this verse, Allāh ﷻ is giving an answer to an individual's mockery of the verses of Allāh ﷻ. Imām Bukhārī ﷺ narrates in his *Ṣaḥīḥ* that during the era of *Jāhiliyyah*, Khabbāb ibn al-'Aratt ؓ was a blacksmith. One *mushrik* by the name of Al-'Āṣ ibn Wā'il Sahmī ordered Khabbāb ؓ to make a sword for him, which he did. Then the *mushrik* refused to pay for it. After repeated begging, Khabbāb ؓ was frustrated and the *mushrik* said, "*I will only pay you on the condition that you denounce Muḥammad and his religion.*"

Khabbāb ؓ said, "*This is not possible, however you must remember that you will die one day and then you will be resurrected,*" The *mushrik* laughed it off and said: "*In that case, when I am resurrected I will be given wealth and children, so I will pay you there.*"

Allāh ﷻ revealed this verse asking how he can be so confident about this? Has he somehow peeped into the unseen and learned of his fate, or has the most merciful Allāh ﷻ, who is not seizing him at the moment, given him some promise?

Then Allāh ﷻ says, "*Never!*" In other words, none of the two things has happened. Rather, we have noted down his words of blasphemy and we shall punish him for it at the correct time and in a proper manner. *Tafsīr Maẓharī* mentions, "*Increasing the punishment means that punishment for rejection is already fixed, however the punishment will be increased for the mockery he has made.*"

"*We will inherit...*" The luxuries of this world are restricted to this *Dunyā*. As soon as a person dies, he is left alone. He goes into his grave without his wealth and without his children. On the day of *Qiyāmah* he will come alone.

One *Ḥadīth* says, "Three things follow a deceased person: his family, his wealth, and his deeds. Then the deeds stay with him, whereas the other two return." [154]

In the case of Al-'Āṣ, his son 'Amr ibn Al-'Āṣ ؓ embraced Islam and went on to be a great warrior and protector of Islam. He supported Islam with the same wealth he had inherited from his father.

---

[154] Mishkāt.

VERSES 81-82

وَاتَّخَذُوْا مِنْ دُوْنِ اللهِ اٰلِهَةً لِّيَكُوْنُوْا لَهُمْ عِزًّا ﴿٨١﴾

كَلَّا ۭ سَيَكْفُرُوْنَ بِعِبَادَتِهِمْ وَيَكُوْنُوْنَ عَلَيْهِمْ ضِدًّا ﴿٨٢﴾

And leaving Allāh aside they adopted many gods, in order that they may be a means of honour for them. Never! They (the gods) will soon reject their worship and will become their adversaries.

"*They adopted many gods...*" The *Mushrikīn* of Makkah had taken many idols for worship. It was *Shayṭān* who whispered in their minds to take them as gods. They would think that these idols would take them closer to God and would intercede on their behalf. They would also think that these idols would bring them power and honour.

"*Never! They will...*" i.e. this will never happen. They will not be honoured nor strengthened by their gods. Rather than interceding for them, their gods will be brought on the day of *Qiyāmah* and they will be given the ability to speak.

They will say:

تَبَرَّأْنَا اِلَيْكَ ز مَا كَانُوْا اِيَّانَا يَعْبُدُوْنَ ۝

"*It is not us that they used to worship.*" [155]

Meaning they used to worship their own imaginations not us. Allāh ﷻ says:

وَيَوْمَ يَحْشُرُهُمْ وَمَا يَعْبُدُوْنَ مِنْ دُوْنِ اللهِ فَيَقُوْلُ ءَاَنْتُمْ اَضْلَلْتُمْ عِبَادِىْ هٰٓؤُلَاءِ اَمْ هُمْ ضَلُّوا السَّبِيْلَ ۝ قَالُوْا سُبْحٰنَكَ مَا كَانَ يَنْبَغِيْ لَنَا اَنْ نَّتَّخِذَ مِنْ دُوْنِكَ مِنْ اَوْلِيَاءَ وَلٰكِنْ

---

[155] Qur'ān 28:63.

مَّتَّعْتَهُمْ وَاٰبَاءَهُمْ حَتّٰى نَسُوا الذِّكْرَ ۚ وَكَانُوْا قَوْمًا بُوْرًا ۝ فَقَدْ كَذَّبُوْكُمْ بِمَا تَقُوْلُوْنَ ۙ

فَمَا تَسْتَطِيْعُوْنَ صَرْفًا وَّلَا نَصْرًا ۝

"The day when He (Allāh) will gather them along with those whom they worshipped leaving aside Allāh, then He will ask (those things they worshipped) "Did you mislead these bondsmen of mine or did they themselves deviate from the path?"

They will reply, "Glory be unto you! It was not befitting for us to take any friends (or protectors) besides you, but what happened was that you granted enjoyment and luxuries to them and to their forefathers until they forgot the reminder, and they were a doomed nation. (Allāh will say) Now that they rejected your claims, you will neither be able to turn away the punishment nor receive any assistance." [156]

Note: كَلَّا is used here. This word appears only in the second half of the Qur'ān. It is used to emphasise the subject matter being discussed before it. Sometimes it is used to deny the claim before it, as in this verse. At other times, it is used to confirm something that follows it, in which case it will be translated as definitely e.g. كَلَّا وَالْقَمَرِ "Surely, by the moon..." [157]

VERSE 83

اَلَمْ تَرَ اَنَّا اَرْسَلْنَا الشَّيٰطِيْنَ عَلَى الْكٰفِرِيْنَ تَؤُزُّهُمْ اَزًّا ﴿٨٣﴾

Have you not seen that We have let loose the shayāṭīn upon the kāfirīn (the deniers) who provoke them tremendously (to commit sin)?

"...We have let loose..." Imām Qurṭubī ﷫ writes, *"This is in reference to when Iblīs asked for the power to lead astray and for respite until the final day."* Allāh replied,

---

[156] Qur'ān 25:17-19.
[157] Al-Muddathir.

"وَاسْتَفْزِزْ مَنِ اسْتَطَعْتَ مِنْهُمْ بِصَوْتِكَ" "And provoke from among them whosoever you can, through your voice..." [158]

تَؤُزُّهُمْ is from 'Azza' which means to pressurise. أَزِيزُ الْمِرْجَلِ means the '*boiling of the pot.*'

VERSE 84

فَلَا تَعْجَلْ عَلَيْهِمْ ۖ إِنَّمَا نَعُدُّ لَهُمْ عَدًّا ﴿٨٤﴾

So do not be hasty against them, We are but counting down for them.

"*We are but counting down...*" Qurṭubī ﷺ says, "*The days, nights, and years.*" Ḍaḥḥāk ﷺ says, "*Their breaths.*" Ibn 'Abbās ﷺ says, "*We count their breaths just as we count their years.*"

Qurṭubī ﷺ narrates that every human being breathes 24,000 times in one day and night, 12,000 during the day and 12,000 during the night.

It is narrated that Al-Ma'mūn recited this *sūrah* and with him were a group of *fuqahā* (jurists). He shook his head towards Ibn Simāk ﷺ indicating to him for some advice.

Ibn Simāk ﷺ said:

إِذَا كَانَتِ الأَنْفَاسُ بِالْعَدَدِ وَلَمْ يَكُنْ لَهَا مَدد فَمَا أَسْرَعَ مَا تَنْفُذُ .

"*When the breaths are being counted, and there is no extra amount to be added, then how quickly will they finish.*"

A poet has said:

حَيَاتُكَ أَنْفَاسٌ تُعَدُّ فَكُلَّمَا . مَضَى نَفَسٌ مِنْكَ اِنْتَقَصْتَ بِهِ جُزْءاً .

"*Your life is the breaths which are counted; whenever one breath passes a part of you has decreased.*"

يُمِيْتُكَ مَا يُحْيِيْكَ فِى كُلِّ لَيْلَةٍ . وَيَحْدُوْكَ حَادٍ مَا يُرِيدُ بِهِ الهَزْءاً .

---

[158] Banī Isrā'īl.

"That very thing which keeps you alive is killing you every night. And a caller is calling upon you and this is no joke."

VERSE 85

يَوْمَ نَحْشُرُ الْمُتَّقِينَ إِلَى الرَّحْمَٰنِ وَفْدًا ﴿٨٥﴾

On the day We will gather those who have Taqwā to Ar-Raḥmān (the All-Merciful) with due ceremony.

"*With due ceremony...*" Like a delegation, who are invited by the king and special limousines are sent to collect them from the airport and special attention is paid towards them.

'Amr ibn Qays Al-Mulā'ī says, "*When a believer will emerge from his grave his good deeds will appear in front of him in a form of a most beautiful person, with the most pleasant aroma. The person will ask*: "*Do you know me?*" *He will reply*: "*No, However Allāh* ﷻ *has gifted you with the most pleasant fragrance and he has beautified your appearance.*" He will say: "*This is how you were in the world, I am your virtuous deeds, for long periods, I used to ride you in the world, now you may ride me.*" Then he recited this verse.

As for the disbeliever, he will be confronted by his deeds in the ugliest form and with the foulest stench. The person will say, "*Do you know me?*" He will reply in the negative saying, "*No, However, Allāh* ﷻ *has made your appearance really ugly and made you malodorous.*" He will reply, "*That is how you were in the world. I am your evil deeds. You very frequently rode on my back in the world so today I shall ride you.*" And he recited, "*... And they will be carrying their burdens on their backs.*"

Tha'labī رحمه الله narrates from 'Alī رضي الله عنه that when this was revealed I said, "*O Messenger of Allāh! I have seen the kings and their delegations, no delegation comes without riding.*" He replied, "*O 'Alī! When the time of returning in the presence of Allāh [comes], the angels will meet the believers with white camels, whose saddles and reigns will be made from gold, upon every ride there will be a suit of clothes which the whole world cannot equal. Every believer will be instructed to wear from those suits. Then the rides will travel with them, the camels will lean forward with them until they arrive at Jannah. The angels there will receive them with the words: "May peace be upon you, you have been cleansed, so come in to stay forever."* [159]

Imām Qurṭubī says, "*This Ḥadīth indicates that this riding will be after the reckoning. However when they come out of their graves, they will be without any footwear and without any clothes, as mentioned in the Ḥadīth.*"

It is possible that some fortunate souls could be given rides as soon as they come out of their graves.

There is a narration from 'Alī that they will not be brought to Allāh on foot, but on camels which will have the saddles made from gold, some will be from red rubies. If they indicate, they will start to walk, and if they move them, they will start flying.

Some *Mufassirīn* say that in the Arabian custom, a delegation normally brings good news and they wait for gifts and presents from the kings, so the *Muttaqīn* will be waiting for gifts and rewards from Allāh.

Verse 86

وَنَسُوقُ الْمُجْرِمِينَ إِلَىٰ جَهَنَّمَ وِرْدًا ﴿٨٦﴾

And we will drive the evildoers to Hell, like cattle to a watering hole.

"*And we will drive...*" The criminals will be driven in a very rough manner, just as when cattle are thirsty and refuse to walk towards a hole filled with water, they have to be moved forcefully until they arrive at the hole and are made to drink.

وِرْدًا - Ibn 'Abbās says, "*This term means thirsty.*" Akhfash and Farrā are of the opinion that it means "*Barefooted and on foot.*" Some say that it means

---

[159] Qur'ān 39.

they will be "*lonely*" while Imām Qurṭubī ﴿ says, "*The word indicates towards thirst because only thirsty one's rush towards water.* [160]

Tafsīr Khāzin narrates from Abū Hurayrah ﴿ that *Rasūlullāh* ﷺ said, "On the day of *Qiyāmah*, people will be gathered in three categories: one group walking, a second one riding, and another group (dragging themselves) on their faces." Someone asked: "*Yā Rasūlallāh*! How will they be able to move on their faces?" He replied: "Surely that Being who made them walk on their feet is able to make them walk on their faces, not just that, they will avert with their faces every thorn and high object." [161]

VERSE 87

لَا يَمْلِكُونَ الشَّفَاعَةَ إِلَّا مَنِ اتَّخَذَ عِنْدَ الرَّحْمْنِ عَهْدًا ﴿٨٧﴾

They will have no right of intercession, none except those who have a contract with Ar-Raḥmān (the All-Merciful).

"*They will have no right if intercession...*" The god fearing and evildoers mentioned above will not have any power over intercession. There will be a time when everyone will be terrified and only worrying about themselves. Then a time will come when Allāh's ﷻ anger will cool down and permission will be granted for intercession. It is at this moment that the golden rule will be announced that intercession will only be allowed for those who have a covenant with Allāh ﷻ, and that is through the *Kalimah*, '*Lā ilāha ill-Allāh*.' So if a person does not have this Kalimah, intercession for him will not be allowed and if someone were to do so, it will not benefit. As Allāh ﷻ says:

فَمَا تَنْفَعُهُمْ شَفَاعَةُ الشَّافِعِينَ ۞

"*Then the intercession of the interceders will not benefit them.*" [162]

---

[160] Tafsīr Qurṭubī, Vol 11, Pg. 153.

[161] Tirmīdhī, Khāzin, Vol 3, Pg. 232.

[162] Qur'ān 74:48.

As for those with the *Kalimah*, the pious will be permitted to speak up and intercede for their loved ones, companions, and for whoever they recognise from their life of the *Dunyā*.

In one *Ḥadīth*, *Rasūlullāh* ﷺ says:

"I will keep interceding until I will say "My Lord! Grant me permission regarding those who have (no good deeds besides the *Kalimah*) *Lā ilāha ill-Allāh Muḥammadur Rasūlullāh*." Allāh will say: "Muḥammad! That is not for you, it is for me only." i.e. only Allāh will be able to recognise their burnt bodies in *Jahannam*."

A *Ḥadīth* says that the '*Ulamā*, *Ḥuffāẓ* and *Ṣulaḥā*' will also be able to intercede. We read in the *Āyah al-Kursī*:

مَنْ ذَا الَّذِيْ يَشْفَعُ عِنْدَهٗٓ اِلَّا بِاِذْنِه ۝

"*Who is he that will intercede before him except with his permission...?*" [163]

VERSE 88

وَقَالُوا اتَّخَذَ الرَّحْمٰنُ وَلَدًا ﴿٨٨﴾

They say: Ar-Raḥmān has taken a son.

"They say, "Ar-Rahman has..." Many people have taken to themselves gods other than Allāh ﷻ, but there were groups who claimed that Allāh ﷻ had taken some of his creation as children. The *Mushrikīn* of Makkah claimed that the Angels were Allāh's ﷻ daughters. Many Jews claimed that 'Uzayr was Allāh's ﷻ son. Most Christians claimed that Allāh ﷻ had taken Ḥadhrat 'Īsā عليه السلام as his son.

[163] Qur'ān 2:255.

Allāh ﷻ has spoken to the Christians at the beginning of the *sūrah*. He has explained very clearly that 'Īsā ﷺ is a Prophet of Allāh ﷻ. In this verse, it seems that Allāh ﷻ is addressing the *Mushrikīn* of Makkah.

VERSE 89

لَّقَدْ جِئْتُمْ شَيْـًٔا اِدًّا ﴿٨٩﴾

So you have definitely devised a monstrous thing.

"So you have definitely..." 'Āllāmah 'Uthmānī رحمه الله writes, "This is such a hideous thing which is spoken and such an insolent word which is uttered that if the heavens, the earth, and the mountains were to split open and be crushed then it would not be any wonder.

Upon this claim Allāh's ﷻ wrath may come into fury then the whole universe may be turned upside down and even the strong heavens and the hard mountains may crush to pieces.

Only Allāh's ﷻ boundless clemency comes in the way that He does not destroy the world upon such claims. How bold is man that he tries to portray Allāh ﷻ as being dependent on children despite the fact that the heavens, the earth, and the mountains and all celestial and earthly objects are witnesses to Allāh's ﷻ divine unity."

VERSES 90-92

تَكَادُ السَّمٰوٰتُ يَتَفَطَّرْنَ مِنْهُ وَتَنْشَقُّ الْاَرْضُ

وَتَخِرُّ الْجِبَالُ هَدًّا ﴿٩٠﴾ اَنْ دَعَوْا لِلرَّحْمٰنِ وَلَدًا ﴿٩١﴾

وَمَا يَنْبَغِىْ لِلرَّحْمٰنِ اَنْ يَّتَّخِذَ وَلَدًا ﴿٩٢﴾

The heavens are really close to being rent apart and the earth to being split open and the mountains are about to be brought crushing down. At their ascription of a son to Ar-Raḥmān. It is not fitting for Ar-Raḥmān to have a son.

"It is not befitting for Raḥmān (The Compassionate One) to have a son..." A question arises here, why does Allāh ﷻ repeat the attribute '*Raḥmān*' in this *sūrah*?

'Ạllāmah 'Ụthmānī ؒ writes that the very idea of having a son is against the dignity and honour of His Holy Self, the glory of His Divine Oneness and the perfection of His Absolute Independence. The purpose, for which the Christians believe the Messiah to be the son is the atonement of sins. This is served easily by the belief in the famous attribute of the All-Compassionate (Raḥmān). And naturally there remains no need to hold the idea and belief of atonement. Allāh is compassionate and extremely merciful, therefore there is no reason to fear any injustice from him nor is there any need for the theory of atonement by devising a son for Him.

Abū Mūsā 'Ash'arī ؓ narrates that *Rasūlullāh* ﷺ said, "None is more tolerant than Allāh ﷻ upon hearing abuse. People attribute children to him, yet he pardons them and continues to feed them." [164]

Abū Hurayrah ؓ narrates that the Prophet ﷺ said that Allāh ﷻ has said, "The son of Ādam says that I am telling a lie, whereas he should not do so. He swears at me, whereas he should not do so. As for his belying, he said that I cannot resurrect him, whereas it is the same for me to create him the second time as I did the first time. His swearing at me is that he says I have children, whereas I am pure from having a wife and children. I am The One, The Independent. I did not give birth to anyone nor did anyone give birth to Me. There is none equal to Me." [165]

VERSE 93

اِنْ كُلُّ مَنْ فِى السَّمٰوٰتِ وَالْاَرْضِ اِلَّآ اٰتِى الرَّحْمٰنِ عَبْدًا ﴿٩٣﴾

There is none in the heavens and the earth but he shall come to Raḥmān as a slave.

---

[164] Mishkāt, Pg. 13.

[165] Ṣaḥīh Al Bukḥārī, Mishkāt, Pg. 13.

"There is none in the heavens and the earth..." This means that whoever is in the heavens and the earth whether man, Jinn, or angel is a servant of God and they shall all appear before Him as servants. So how can a servant become a son? When the whole of the creation are subjects, and dependent on Allāh ﷻ, then why would Allāh ﷻ need to take anyone as a son?

VERSE 94

لَقَدْ اَحْصٰىهُمْ وَعَدَّهُمْ عَدًّا ﴿٩٤﴾

He has counted them all and numbered them all precisely.

"He has counted them..." Allāh ﷻ has perfect knowledge of every single one of his creations and none of them will be able to escape Him on the Day of Judgement. Everyone will be alone. At that time all connections, relations and all means and provisions shall be frozen. Imaginary gods and sons shall not avail at all.

VERSE 95

وَكُلُّهُمْ اٰتِيْهِ يَوْمَ الْقِيٰمَةِ فَرْدًا ﴿٩٥﴾

And every one of them will appear before Him on the day of Qiyāmah all alone.

Maulānā 'Abdul Mājid Daryabādī رحمه الله writes, "It is with the irreplaceable singleness of his individuality that the finite ego will approach the infinite ego to see for himself the consequences of his past actions and to judge the possibilities of his future."

All alone means one will have no helper, no support, no refuge besides Allāh ﷻ alone who has no partners who will judge for His creation how He wills. He is fair and just. He does not do injustice of even an atom's weight nor does He oppress anyone.

VERSE 96

إِنَّ الَّذِينَ ءَامَنُوا وَعَمِلُوا الصَّلِحَتِ سَيَجْعَلُ لَهُمُ الرَّحْمَنُ وُدًّا ﴿٩٦﴾

Surely those who have Īmān and do good acts, Ar-Raḥmān the Most Gracious will bestow love and affection for them.

Tafsīr Mājidī states that such people will be blessed with love in this world as well as the reward in the future. Allāh ﷻ will bless them with His own love and with the esteem of mankind. This was well illustrated in the life of *Rasūlullāh* ﷺ himself who was surrounded by a warm and self-sacrificing love. [166] He also possessed a still and great gift of attaching men to himself. [167]

Ibn Kathīr رحمه الله says this is reported in the authentic *Ḥadīth* narrated by Imām Aḥmad رحمه الله on the authority of Abū Hurayrah رضي الله عنه that *Rasūlullāh* ﷺ said, "Verily, whenever Allāh loves a servant of His, He calls Jibrā'īl and says, "O Jibrā'īl, verily I love so-and-so, so love him." Thus, Jibrā'īl will love him. Then Jibrā'īl will call out to the dwellers of the heavens, "Verily Allāh loves so-and-so, so you too must love him." Then the dwellers of the heavens will love him and he will be given acceptance in the earth. Whenever Allāh dislikes a servant of His, He calls Jibrā'īl and says, "O Jibrā'īl, verily I hate so-and-so, so dislike him." Thus, Jibrā'īl will dislike him. Then, he (Jibrā'īl) will call out amongst the dwellers of the heavens, "Verily, Allāh dislikes so and so, so you too must dislike him." Then the dwellers of the heavens dislike him and hatred for him will be placed in the earth.

Ibn Abī Ḥatim رحمه الله narrates from Abū Hurayrah رضي الله عنه that *Rasūlullāh* ﷺ said, "Whenever Allāh loves a servant of his, he calls Jibrā'īl (saying), "Verily I love so and so, so love him." Then Jibrā'īl calls out into the heavens and love for him descends among the people of the earth. That is the meaning of the statement of Allāh ﷻ, the Mighty and Sublime, "Verily, those who believe

[166] Muir, Pg. 513.

[167] McDonald Aspects of Islam, Pg. 74.

and perform deeds of righteousness, the Most Gracious will bestow love for them..." [168]

Imām Aḥmad رحمه الله narrated from Thowbān رضي الله عنه that *Rasūlullāh* ﷺ said, "Surely a person seeks the pleasure of Allāh and continues to do so until Allāh says to Jibrā'īl, "Surely so and so is my servant, he seeks to please me, lo My mercy is upon him." So Jibrā'īl replies, "Allāh's mercy is upon so and so." The Angels carrying the throne also say, "May Allāh's *raḥmah* be on so and so." Until the dwellers of the seven heavens say it and it descends upon the land."

وُدًّا means 'Love'. Mujāhid رحمه الله says this means love in the hearts of people in the *Dunyā*. Sa'īd ibn Jubayr رحمه الله says, "Allāh ﷻ loves these people and creates their love in the hearts of believers." Ibn 'Abbās رضي الله عنهما says, "Muslims love them in the *Dunyā* and Allāh ﷻ provides goodly provisions for them and gives them good names."

Qatādah رحمه الله says, "*Wallāh* this is the love in the hearts of the faithful people. We have been told that Ḥaram ibn Ḥayyān used to say that whenever a person turns to Allāh ﷻ wholeheartedly, Allāh ﷻ turns the heart of the faithful towards them, and then Allāh ﷻ blesses him with their love and affection." Qatādah says, "Ụthmān ibn 'Ạffān رضي الله عنه used to say, "*No servant does any good or bad deed but Allāh ﷻ covers him with the sheet of his actions.*"

VERSE 97

فَإِنَّمَا يَسَّرْنَٰهُ بِلِسَانِكَ لِتُبَشِّرَ بِهِ ٱلْمُتَّقِينَ وَتُنذِرَ بِهِۦ قَوْمًا لُّدًّا ﴿٩٧﴾

We have made the Qur'ān easy in your own language so that you may give glad tidings to those who have Taqwā and warn the quarrelsome people.

Ibn Kathīr mentions that the language of the Prophet ﷺ is eloquent, clear, and complete Arabic.

---

[168] This was also reported by Muslim and Tirmīdhī.

اَلَّ here means those who are crooked from the truth and who have turned towards falsehood. Mujāhid ؓ says, "They are people who never walk straight." Ḍaḥḥāk ؓ says, "Al-Alad refers to a severely argumentative person." Al-Qurzi ؓ states, "Al-Alad is in reference to the fabricator (liar)." Ḥasan Baṣrī ؓ says, "It means to be deaf of heart." Others say, "Their hearts are deaf." Ibn 'Abbās ؓ says, "اَلَّ means 'Fujjāran' (transgressors)." Ibn Zaid ؓ says, "Al-Alad means 'the tyrant'."

Maulānā Idrīs Kāndhalwī ؓ writes that it is to be noted here that Maqbūlīyyah and Maḥbūbīyyāt (being accepted and being loved) by Allāh ﷻ is different to shuhrah (fame). Love starts from the pious and God fearing people. Allāh ﷻ places the love in the hearts of the God fearing and gradually, general acceptance is given to such people. Being famous in the media or due to some leadership or other reasons is not a sign of being accepted in the eyes of Allāh ﷻ.

VERSE 98

$$\text{وَكَمْ اَهْلَكْنَا قَبْلَهُمْ مِّنْ قَرْنٍ ۚ هَلْ تُحِسُّ}$$

$$\text{مِنْهُمْ مِّنْ اَحَدٍ اَوْ تَسْمَعُ لَهُمْ رِكْزًا ﴿٩٨﴾}$$

How many were the generations that We destroyed before them. Do you see any of them or do you hear any whisper from them?

The meaning of this final āyah is clear, it is a warning from Allāh ﷻ that many generations have been destroyed and you could suffer the same fate as well.

The Mushrikīn could also suffer a similar fate.

Ibn 'Abbās, 'Ikrimah and Abūl 'Āliya say رِكْزَا means: 'Sautan' which means: 'whisper'. Literally رِكْزَا means faint voice.

Allāh ﷻ gives respite to the transgressors. However, when He seizes, He does not let go. This was the condition of the previous kuffār but we see today that the apparent condition of many Muslims is also similar with regards to arguing, lying, cheating, committing fraud, etc.

May Allāh ﷻ have mercy upon us and give us the tawfīq and ability to perform good deeds and May Allāh ﷻ gives us a good ending with *Īmān. Āmīn*

BIBLIOGRAPHY

1. *Jāmi' Tirmīdhī*

By Abū 'Īsā Muḥammad ibn 'Īsā ibn Sawrah al-Tirmīdhī ﵀ (d.279 AH). The *Jāmi'* of Imām al-Tirmīdhī ﵀ ranks third among the *Ṣiḥāḥ Sittah* (the six authentic books of *Ḥadīth*).

2. *Ma'ārif al-Qur'ān*

A lengthy but heart-warming and satisfying commentary of the Holy Qur'ān in the Urdu language. There are two *Tafsīrs* with the same name, but by different authors: (1) Muftī Shafī Ṣāḥib ﵀, (2) Maulānā Idrīs Kāndhalwī Ṣāḥib ﵀. I have used that of Maulānā Idrīs Kāndhalwī Ṣāḥib ﵀ because I found it more comprehensive and due it being enough to quench my thirst. It consists of eight lengthy volumes.

3. *Faḍā'il-e-Ṣadaqah*

By *Sheikh al-Ḥadīth* Maulānā Muḥammad Zakarīyyā' ﵀.

4. *Maẓāhir-e-Ḥaqq*

A commentary of *Mishkāt al-Maṣābīḥ*, which is the famous collection of *Ḥadīth*. The author is Nawāb Muḥammad Quṭb ad-Dīn Khān Dehlavī ﵀ who was among the students of Shah 'Abd al-'Azīz Muḥaddith Dehlavī ﵀.

5. *Mishkāt al-Maṣābīḥ*

By Muḥammad ibn 'Ạbdullāh ﵀, well known as Khatīb Tabrezī ﵀. He gathered a fine compilation of 5945 *Aḥādīth*. (d. 740 AH).

6. *Rūḥ al-Ma'ānī*
By 'Ạllāmah Alūsī Baghdādī ﷫. A very comprehensive *Tafsīr* consisting of various topics especially *tasawwuf.* He was a Ḥanafī Scholar, thus he supports the Ḥanafī research in *Masā'il.*

7. *Ṣaḥīh al-Bukhḥārī*
The famous *Muḥaddith*, Muḥammad ibn Ismā'īl Bukhḥārī ﷫ or I should say *Amīrul Mu'minīn Fī al-Ḥadīth* as my teacher Shaykh Yūnus Ṣāḥib ﷫ used to say whenever he would start the discourses of *Ṣaḥīḥ al-Bukhḥārī.* He died in the year 194 AH. His book is well known for *Ṣaḥīḥ Aḥādīth* although this does not mean that all the other *Aḥādīth* are false, rather it simply means he has put forward a good collection of authentic *Aḥādīth.*

8. *Ṣaḥīḥ Muslim*
Also a famous *Muḥaddith*, Muslim ibn Ḥajjāj ibn Muslim al-Qusharī an-Naisāpūrī ﷫ (d.206 AH). He followed in the footsteps of Imām Bukhḥārī ﷫. He also acquired from Imām Bukhḥārī ﷫ a considerable amount of knowledge in the field of *Asmā Wa al-Rijāl* (the science related to investigating the condition of each narrator in the chain of *Aḥādīth*).

9. *Sunan Abū Dāwūd*
By Sulaimān ibn Ash'ath al-Sijistānī ﷫ (d. 257 AH).

10. *Sunan Ibn Mājah*
By 'Ạbdullāh Muḥammad ibn Yazīd ibn Mājah al-Qazwīnī ﷫ (d.273 AH).

11. *Tafsīr Ibn Kathīr*
By Ḥāfiẓ Imām ad-Dīn Ismā'īl ibn 'Umar ibn Kathīr ad-Dimishqī ﷫. I would say that without doubt he is the number one commentator and no one can even come close to him. *Tafsīr* just flows from his pen like water gushing out of a fountain. He is the most authentic commentator

in the sense that he only narrates the sound *Aḥādīth* and refrains from narrating any fabricated *Aḥādīth*. Also, another beauty of his work is '*Tafsīr al-Qur'ān bi al-Qur'ān*' i.e. he brings forth verses similar to the ones in connection, from different *sūrahs* of the Qur'ān.

As-Suyūṭī has said, "*No Tafsīr like it has been compiled.*" 'Allāmah Anwar Shah Kashmīrī is said to have commentated that Ibn Kathīr has done nothing but shortened the *Tafsīr* of Ibn Jarīr at-Ṭabarī. However, many of the scholars say that this is not correct because Ibn Kathīr has increased it with many beneficial comments, which do not appear in Ibn Jarīr's version. Ibn Kathīr passed away on 15th Sha'bān 774 AH. He was buried in the graveyard of the *Sūfīyāh*, alongside his Sheikh, Imām Ibn Taymīyyah.

12. *Tafsīr Khāzin*

The author of this *Tafsīr* is known as 'Ạlī ibn Muḥammad ibn Ibrāhīm al-Baghdādī al-Shafi'ī al-Sūfī (d.741 AH), well known by the title 'Khāzin'. He completed his *Tafsīr* on 10th Ramaḍān 725 AH. The original name of the *Tafsīr* is '*Lubāb at-Ta'wīl Fī Ma'ānī at-Tanzīl*'. It is a very good compilation of Prophetic narrations, jurisprudence, lexical research, and *taṣawwuf*. However, one has to be cautious in taking narrations from it.

13. *Tafsīr Mājidī*

A commentary of the Holy Qur'ān compiled by Ḥaḍhrat Maulānā 'Abdul Mājid Daryabādī (d. 1973). Ḥaḍhrat Maulānā was educated in various universities in India. He has put a great effort in giving references from the gospels.

14. *Tafsīr 'Ụthmānī*

A footnote type commentary of the Holy Qur'ān by 'Ạllāmah Shabbīr Aḥmad 'Ụthmānī – Short, simple and informative.

14. *Translation of the Holy Qur'ān*

By Abdullāh Yūsuf Alī, probably the most famous English translator and commentator of the Holy Qur'ān. However, one has to be cautious in narrating from him. He never mentions the name of any previous commentators; sometimes he uses words which shock the reader. A book entitled, 'Errors of Abdullāh Yūsuf Alī' has been published in South Africa.

15. *Qur'ān made easy – Translation of the Holy Qur'ān*

This is an English translation of the Holy Qur'ān in contemporary English to make reading much easier and more understandable.

16. *Tafsīr Al-Qurṭubī*

A classical commentary of the Holy Qur'ān. Imām Abū 'Ạbdullāh Muḥammad ibn Aḥmad ibn Abū Bakr al-Anṣārī al-Qurṭubī رحمه الله, who was born in Cordoba, Spain. He was an eminent Mālikī Scholar who specialised in *Fiqh* and *Ḥadīth* (d.671 AH).

GLOSSARY

A

Ākhirah: Hereafter
Alḥamdulillāh: All praises are due to Allāh ﷻ
'Ālim: Islamic Scholar
Āmīn: O Allāh ﷻ accept our invocation
Aqīdah: Beliefs
Āyah/Āyāt (plural): Verse
Ạdhāb: Punishment
Adhān: Call to prayer

D

Du'ā: Supplication
Dunyā: World

F

Farḍh/Farā'iḍ: Compulsory
Fiqh: The understanding and application of Islamic ideas, laws, commandments etc. from original source of Sharīạ.

H

Ḥadīth: (Plural: Aḥādīth) originally means a piece of news, story, or a report relating to a past or present event. In the technical meaning, it stands for the report of the words and deeds, approval and dispproval of *Rasūlullāh* ﷺ. In other words, the saying, action or consent of *Rasūlullāh* ﷺ.

Ḥajj: Pilgrimage
Ḥalāl: Lawful, permissible
Hidāyah: Guidance
Ḥisāb: Account

I

'Ịbādah: Worship
'Ịlm: Knowledge
Imām: The person who leads others in *Ṣalāh* (Prayer) or Muslim Caliph (Ruler)
Īmān: Faith
Inshā Allāh': If Allāh ﷻ wills

J

Jahannam: Hell
Jāhil: Ignorant
Jalāl: Great, Exalted, Greatness, Superiority
Jannah/Jannat: Paradise

K

Kāfir: Disbelievers, Rejecters
Khushū': Sincerity
Khuṭbah: Sermon

M

Majlis: Gathering
Makkah: The holiest city of Islam
Malak al-Maut: Angel of Death
Masā'il: Issues/Queries

Mufassirīn: Commentators of the Holy Qur'ān
Muqtadīs: People following the Imām
Mushrikīn: Polytheist, Pagans, Idolaters and Disbelievers in the oneness of Allāh ﷻ
Mustaḥab: Agreeable, Desirable, Liked
Mu'tazilah: A cult born in the first Islamic century, which gained popularity among the 'Ạbbāsid Khulafā. Their main difference with the Ahl as-Sunnah was to give preference with the 'Aql (logic) over Naql (Narrations). They also had some differences in Aqīdah.

N

Nabi: Prophet
Nafl: Optional
Nubūwwah: Prophethood

Q

Qaḍā': Making up for missed prayers/fasts etc.
Qurb: Closeness

R

Rabb: Lord
Raḥmah: Mercy
Rasūl: Messenger

S

Ṣadaqah: Charity, Alms giving
Ṣaḥābah: The noble companions ﷺ of the Holy Prophet ﷺ who saw him and believed him.

Ṣaḥīḥ Ḥadīth: Authentic tradition in text and chain
Ṣalāh: Prayer
Ṣawm: Fasting
Sharīạ: Islamic Code
Shirk: Polytheism, to worship any other deity than Allāh ﷻ
Ṣiddīq: Truthful
Sūrah: Chapter of the Qur'ān

T

Tafsīr: Exegesis, most often used to describe the commentary of the Holy Qur'ān
Tahajjud: *Ṣalāh* performed at night, the best time for which is the last portion of the night, between four and twelve rak'ah
Taqwā: Piety, constant awareness of Allāh ﷻ
Tawbah: Repentance

U

Ummah: Nation

W

Waḥī: Revelations from Allāh ﷻ
Wuḍū': Ablution

Y

Ya'jūj Ma'jūj: Gog Magog

Z

Zakāh: Charity, 2.5 percent of surplus wealth, which a Muslim should give to the poor, once a year
Dhikr: Remembrance of Allāh ﷻ
Zinā: Adultery